The Translation of Nosso
Our Guiding Principles

D0113324

Sensus non verba (Meaning not words)
Cicero

The Translation and Editorial Team has seen the challenge of translating *Nosso Lar* from its original Portuguese in two ways. We might best describe them metaphorically.

Imagine that two individuals have been invited to give the same talk to different audiences. The first speaker takes the theme to heart, delves into its ideas, convinces himself of its facts, and when on stage, speaks with a profound conviction, allowing his audience to share in his emotions to the extent that it enthusiastically affirms every major point, and endorses his conclusions. This audience is captivated by the ideas, applauds warmly, and avidly seeks to learn more from the speaker during the break.

The second speaker delivers basically the same speech—where content is concerned—but uses a methodical approach, lacks humor and feeling, and speaks in a monotone. The audience stays to the end, applauds respectfully, and quietly heads for the exits.

Always our challenge has been to make sure that the audience for *Nosso Lar*, which will come hoping for the first kind of experience, will not find itself surprised—and disappointed—by the second kind. Both presentations may be correct in their details; only one is memorable.

Thus, from the outset we sought to deliver an experience like our first example, one wherein the book's emotions, expressions, attitudes, and personalities would have the same liveliness, power, and meaning for modern American readers as the original work had for its Brazilian ones. This was particularly critical in the reproduction of dialogue. Here we wanted to carry over the tension, rhythm, and flow of the original Portuguese into English idioms—a task that demanded a good deal of creativity since differences in grammatical structure and levels of precision between Portuguese and English are often dramatic. Further, we sought to recreate the dialogues in a way that reflected both the spoken language of contemporary America and at the same maintained the high literary quality that marks the best current books in this country.

The difficulties of such an enterprise are the same that have confronted literary translators since Cicero and Quintilian, and have concerned those who have written about the art and theory of translation for over two thousand years. The approach we chose decidedly avoided the literal, strict word-for-word matching, or the other extreme, that of adaptation or free interpretation. Instead, we embraced what Dryden established as the high road and called *paraphrase*, 'or (the process of) translation with latitude, where the author is kept in view by the translator, so as never to be lost, but his words are not so strictly followed as his sense, and that too is admitted to be amplified, but not altered'.[1]

Thus, we have tried in these pages to eliminate anything that by its cultural and linguistic particularity would create a barrier between our American readers and the book's message. The content is completely faithful to the ideas and observations of André Luiz, as he communicated them in the early '40s; we hope that the reader will find, however, that this work speaks directly to his or her soul today in an unaffected manner that avoids the stylistic stiffness of much translated work. We wanted to offer you a book as André Luiz might have written it had he been writing in English—a book that would evoke in the American reader the same feelings of reverence, faith, and spiritual comfort experienced by the readers of the original. This, we believe, is that book.

This is *not*, then, the work of translators in the strictest sense of the word, but our expression of a powerful experience by inspired writers and poetic souls. We hope you enjoy the experience.

The Editorial Team

----

[1] Cited in George Steiner, *After Babel: Aspects of Language and Translation* (Oxford University Press, 1998), p. 269. For a full discussion of Dryden's position the author makes reference to W. Frost, *Dryden and the Art of Translation* (Yale University Press, 1955).

Preface

This is no ordinary novel. It is not a romantic adventure produced by the prolific mind of a gifted fiction writer. This is the first book dictated by André Luiz, a discarnate soul, to Francisco C. Xavier, one of the most productive mediums and inspirational writers of our time. In this partnership, André Luiz acts as a reporter on conditions in the spirit world, revealing details of its life, people, places, and organization. He does so through the lens of his reflections on his own after-death experience, and his struggles to make sense of his new reality. In this very personal account, André Luiz reveals his identity as a medical doctor who practiced in southeastern Brazil in the first decades of the twentieth century, and who left the physical body a few years prior to the beginning of World War II. A true skeptic at the time of his demise, he is initially shocked at the discovery that death is nothing more than a doorway to a new and richer life. As time progresses, however, he undergoes inevitable experiences and teachings in the spirit realm which lead him to a better understanding of life's meaning.

André Luiz's, or Andy's, account of life in the spiritual realm is profoundly linked to his acceptance of God as the architect and creator of our Universe. This book, and the many others that have since followed, have all been dictated in Portuguese, and have guided hundreds of thousands of readers toward a more profound understanding of the reality that lies beyond. They have been dictated through the extraordinary paranormality of Francisco C. Xavier (1910 -), who has co-authored over 350 books in almost seventy years of unconditional dedication to Christ's cause on Earth. Born to a poor family and possessing only an elementary school education he has become one of the most prolific contributors to the development of the Spiritist philosophy. The profits resulting from his vast

literary production have been donated to charities and non-profit
organizations in Brazil.

The first edition of Nosso Lar was translated by Mr. Salim
Haddad, and published in 1986 under the title Astral City by the
Christian Spirit Center in North Carolina. A man of great spiritual
culture and evangelical humility, Mr. Haddad was the first champi-
on of the Christian Spiritist way of life in the United States, and the
English editor of many other books by F. C. Xavier. This new translation is a child of Mr. Haddad's own desire to offer the American public a book that would capture, in a vibrant, contemporary language,
the deepest emotional content of Andre Luiz's awakening. In Mr.
Haddad's conception, this language, while faithful to the original
content, would bring the reader into that realm of nearly inexpressible emotions that the soul experiences when it looks into itself. This
new translation has the vision and touch of poetry that only poets
can render when they drink from a book about the essential divinity of life.

The editors of this new translation recognize that Mr. Haddad's
concern was well placed when he realized that a blind adherence to
the linguistic structure of the original work had dulled the soul of
the book. In 1991, when he gave the AKES the original electronic
files, he invited us to produce a new edition that "moistened the eyes
and lifted the reader's imagination to the sublimity of life and God."
We believe we have come as close to his vision as possible, stretch-
ing to the utmost our ability to dress with words the language of the
soul. Unfortunately, Providence had other plans for Mr. Haddad,
who passed on a few months after his giving his gift and who thus
did not see the completion of this project. This book is dedicated in
his honor and to his memory.

The time has come for Andre Luiz's very real experiences to
become public in all corners of the globe, reaching readers that only
English, the most widely spread of languages, could hope to touch.
This translation is the culmination of eight years of intense and
detailed work by volunteers and friends of the Allan Kardec
Educational Society. We are indebted to Daniel Benjamin, Brenda
Haney, Antulio Bonfim, Elza d'Agosto, Rosalinda Fly, Lucia
Machado-Schedig, Ivan Moraes, Jeanne and Paul Murphy, and
Miriam Wilcox, and others too many to list here, who patiently and,
more often than not, repeatedly, reviewed and revised, suggested
and helped, offering many hours of their personal time to this

endeavor. Dr. Robert Champ bravely edited and unearthed the hidden sparkle from the first English version. Nothing could have been done without the loving, steering hand of Dr. John Zerio, who passionately offered much more than selfless and complete dedication to the Nosso Lar project. In addition, we thank the executive board of FEB (Federação Espirita Brasileira), and are grateful especially for the support of Mr. Altivo Ferreira, Lauro São Tiago, Nestor Masotti, and Mr. Juvanir Borges de Sousa, President. A special recognition goes to Mr. Jose Yosan Fonseca, assistant to the President, who led the revision work for FEB.

As we, the Allan Kardec Educational Society, offer this work to you, the reader, it is our hope that we have honored the love—the true spirit of life—that inspired André Luiz and F. C. Xavier. If this work brings you a new vision of reality we'll feel that this effort was not in vain; if you want to share your thoughts with us, please write to us at AKES, or visit our web site: http://www.allan-kardec.org.

Andrea Dessen, Ph. D.
Project Director

Preface by Emmanuel

A NEW FRIEND

*P*refaces generally introduce authors, extolling their virtues and enlarging on their personalities. Here, however, the situation is different. There are no earthly records for a physician named André Luiz.

Often real understanding and true love come to us hidden under the cloak of anonymity. In order to redeem an unpleasant past in the process of reincarnation, old names are wiped away and new ones take their places. All past events sink into temporary oblivion—a blessing of Divine Mercy.

In this way, a curtain has been drawn over André Luiz's former self. Thus we cannot introduce an earthly doctor and human writer, but instead present a new friend and brother in eternity.

In order to bring his valuable impressions to earthly friends, it was necessary for him to forego all conventions, including the use of his name. He did so to avoid hurting loved ones still wrapped in the mist of illusion. The experienced farmer who has rich harvests knows to respect the newly planted land as wells the green fields still in bloom.

We realize that this book is not the only one of its kind. Others have already described the conditions of life beyond the grave. Nevertheless, we are glad to have drawn to our spiritual circles one who might transmit an account of his own experiences. He gives as much detail as possible to clarify the laws that preside over the efforts of diligent spirits of good will in spheres which though invis-

ible to human eyes, are intimately connected with this planet.
Many will surely smile on reading certain passages in this narra-
tive. Let me remind you, however, that the unusual always causes
surprise. Who on the Earth did not smile tolerantly upon hearing
about aviation, electricity, or the radio before their development
some decades ago?

Surprise, perplexity and doubt are common to students who have
not yet gone over their lessons: that is only natural and most just. Yet
we would not think of criticizing our neighbor's point of view,
although we might disagree with it. Every reader must analyze for
himself what he reads.

We will refer here to the essential aim of this work. The Spiritist
Doctrine is rapidly increasing the number of its adepts. Thousands
of people are taking interest in its work, methods and experiments.
Yet, faced with a world of novelties, human beings must not neglect
their most important goal—their own spiritual growth.

It is not enough to investigate phenomena, adhere verbally to any
doctrine, collect and improve statistics, exhort the conscience of others, gain converts, or win public approval—however commendable
all this may be on the physical plane. It is essential to acquire the
knowledge about our infinite potential, and to use it in the service of
good.

Human beings aren't forsaken on Earth. They are children of God
engaged in constructive work, temporarily clothed in flesh. They are
students in a meritorious school, where they must learn to raise
themselves up. The human struggle is their opportunity, their set of
tools and their textbook.

Interchange with the invisible is a sacred movement, functioning
to restore pure Christianity. Let no one neglect his own obligations
in the place he occupies by the Lord's design.

André Luiz comes to tell us, dear reader, that the greatest surprise
of bodily death is that it places us face-to-face with our own consciences, where we build our heaven, remain in purgatory, or plunge
ourselves into the infernal abysses. He reminds us that the Earth is
our sacred school which no one should desecrate without knowing
the price of this terrible mistake.

Keep his lessons in the book of your soul. They remind us that it
is not enough for human beings to cling to their human existence. It
is necessary to know how to use that existence worthily. The steps of

a Christian, whatever his religious affiliation, should move truly toward Christ. To this end we have great need of the Spiritist Doctrine, but most of all Spirituality.

Emmanuel[1]

City of Pedro Leopoldo, October 3, 1943.

----

[1] *Translators' Note: Emmanuel is the spirit guide of Francisco C. Xavier. Emmanuel's life and reincarnation experiences on Earth are recounted in several books received by the same author among them: Two Thousand Years Past, Fifty Years Later, Sacrifice of Love. These works are in process of translation by AKES.*

Introduction

$\mathcal{A}$ MESSAGE FROM ANDRÉ LUIZ

$\mathcal{L}$ife never ends. It is an everflowing source, and death is only the artful effect of an illusion.

A great river follows its own course before emptying into the vast sea. Likewise, the soul follows equally varied courses and passes through different banks—receiving here and there tributaries of knowledge, strengthening its identity and perfecting its qualities — before reaching the Ocean of Eternal Wisdom.

The closing of our earthly eyes is such a simple event.

The shedding of the physical body doesn't solve the fundamental questions of awareness, just as changing one's clothes has nothing to do with the deep questions of life and destiny.

Paths of the soul ... mysterious ways of the heart ... we must walk their full length before we face the supreme equation of Eternal Life. It is indispensable for us to live all of our challenges, to fully know ourselves in the long process of spiritual ascent.

How childish it is to imagine that the mere "ringing down of the curtain" could settle transcendental questions about the Infinite.

One life is but a single act.

One body — a garment.

One century — a day.

One task — an experience.

One triumph — an acquisition.

One death — a breath of renewal.

How many lives, bodies, centuries, tasks, triumphs, and deaths are still allotted to us? And yet religious philosophers continue to talk about final decisions and definitive situations. Unfortunately, everywhere we find religious scholars who are spiritual illiterates.

It takes a great effort for one to enter the School of the Gospel, and admission to it usually comes to pass through uncommon means. The seeker finds him or herself alone with the Master, toiling through a difficult curriculum, learning lessons in an invisible class-room, and attending long, silent lectures.

It is a hard journey, and a long one; very long. Our contribution here, then, humble as it is, can give you only a glimpse of this fundamental reality. Indeed, I am grateful for the opportunity!

I speak to you as an anonymous friend, in an anonymity that stems from brotherly love. Humanity is like a fragile vessel which cannot, as yet, contain the whole truth. Thus, we restrict ourselves here to conveying only the essence of the soul's experience in its more encompassing values. We will not try to impose on anyone the idea of Eternity. First, let the vessels become stronger. We dedicate this brief record to the eager souls of our brothers and sisters who are struggling for spiritual ascent, and who understand, as we do, that "the wind blows wherever it pleases."[2]

And now, my friends, let my gratitude be recorded in these pages as a silent testimonial of my sympathy and thankfulness. Friendship, sympathy, love, and happiness live in the soul. Be sure that in the depths of mine I hold these feelings toward you, the reader.

May God bless us.

André Luiz

---

[2]*Translator's Note: John 3:8 "The wind blows wherever it pleases. You hear its sound, but you cannot tell where it comes from or where it is going. So it is with everyone born of the Spirit."*

[3]*Translator's Note: This a pen name adopted, as explained by the author in other communications, to prevent his earthly reputation from interfering with the readers' experience, or preventing the ideas from standing on their own merit.*

Chapter One[4]

IN THE LOWER ZONE

I had lost all sense of space and time.

I was still breathing—swallowing great gulps of air—but it didn't matter. Because if there was one thing I was sure of with absolute certainty, it was this: I wasn't alive anymore. Not in the usual sense of the word, anyway.

I couldn't tell where I was, but it seemed to me that somewhere along the line I had been overtaken by irresistible forces, and that I was their pawn.

I felt as trapped as a prisoner does in his cell—and a dark cell at that, filled with horrors. Sometimes, as I moved around, the fear was so intense that my heart raced wildly, almost bursting.

Often I would scream like a madman — begging for mercy and crying out in protest at the despair gripping my spirit. But those cries fell on deaf ears, or would be answered by even more pitiful cries, coming from the darkness around me. At times evil-sounding laughter would shatter the silence, making me believe that an unknown companion was also a prisoner of this madness, caught in the same horrific nightmare.

From time to time, scary forms and faces passed before me. I could barely make them out, but they were there—visible in the

----

[4]*Translator's Note: Some names have been literally translated; in a few instances the editors have adopted the closest sounding equivalent. The author uses very rare and sometimes strangely sounding names in Portuguese to save people, according to him, from wasting their time hunting clues to the characters' identities or placing actual people in the situations he describes. He adopted this approach to facilitate the reading experience, and to increase retention of the lessons he intended the reader to take away from that experience.*

lurid light that at times washed over that place, so that it seemed covered in a thick fog lit by a few rays of sunlight. In this way, my strange, hurried and stumbling journey continued—to where, I couldn't tell. I only knew I had to keep moving; that fear was driving me, pushing me this way and that. I had lost all sense of direction. I couldn't think straight any more. The fear of the unknown had paralyzed my mind from the moment I had broken free of my physical bonds in the grave.

If only this had been all. But at the same time, in the midst of all this fear, my conscience burned inside me. Better, I thought, if I were simply non-existent. Instead, I found myself crying constantly. Rest came rarely and even then only for a few minutes, for invariably it was interrupted by the ghastly beings who laughed and mocked at me.

And all the time, through all these constant horrors, I kept thinking: My God, is this real? Where is my house? Where are my wife and children?

And I ran on.

Bewildering thoughts clashed in my mind. After a while the realization came that I was, in fact, on a different plane of life—a plane that arose in some way from the emanations of Earth itself. Unfortunately, it was a realization that came too late to do me any good in my present situation. Besides, my mind was so tormented that, whenever I tried to make some sense of my situation, so many confusing things happened in sequence that I would soon get lost in a labyrinth of thoughts.

There was one area, though, where my thinking took on a new clarity.

I had never before concerned myself with religious questions; now they loomed large before me. The political, philosophical, and scientific ideas that had always been of such value to me on Earth now seemed trivial. I saw them suddenly as quite transitory. It struck me forcibly that humanity isn't composed of transitory beings. Human beings are, rather, immortal spirits engaged in a great ascent, and bound to attain a glorious destination. I began to realize, too, the existence of one thing that stands above all material and intellectual values: the divine revelation of Faith.

Yet as I say, such perceptions had come too late. True, while on

Earth, I was familiar enough with the Old Testament and had often read through the Gospel. So why these current circumstances? I was forced to realize that I had never really searched the scriptures by the light of my heart. Instead, I had accepted interpretations of them by writers who lacked real discernment, had no reverence for them and sometimes openly disagreed with the basic truths. At other times I had let the Church do the thinking for me, and thus never broke away from the circle of contradictions in which I stood of my own volition.

I had not been exactly an evil-doer in my earthly life, I thought. Yet my philosophy of living for the immediate present had occupied all of my attention. And in this I wasn't so different from a great many others.

I had been born to parents who had spoiled me, had graduated from medical school without major sacrifices, and had taken part in the vices of the youth of my generation. Later, I had married and started a family. I subsequently carved out a stable and well-paying practice for myself and had no financial worries. Yet, looking inward here in this new place, I began to realize that I had squandered my time—and with that thought the silent pangs of conscience came to trouble me. I had lived on Earth, enjoyed its benefits, reaped the good things of life—yet I had never added much toward the repayment of the heavy debt I owed for all these gifts. I had completely ignored my parents' generosity and sacrifices. I had selfishly kept my family to myself alone. I had been given a happy home; but when anyone had come to me in need of help, I had more often than not been indifferent. I had delighted in the joys of my family, yet never shared it with my larger, human family. I had neglected even the simplest duties of brotherhood.

Now my life was over, and I was like a greenhouse plant that is suddenly taken outdoors: that is, I was wilting in the weather of eternal realities. God had sown divine seeds in my soul; I hadn't cultivated them. Instead, my endless desires for material comfort and pleasure had choked them.

Certainly, I wasn't prepared for the new life I was leading. I had entered it as someone without arms or legs who is thrown into the infinite river of eternity and cannot prevent himself from rolling with the water; or like a frail wanderer lost in a desert storm. And, I had to conclude, it was only right that this should be so.

My friends of earth... you can avoid the course of agony I've just described—but only if you tend to the inner fields of your soul. Before you cross over into the Shadow of Death, light up your inner lamp. Search for the truth, or it will find you unprepared. Work with all your might now, or you will cry—as I did—afterwards.

Chapter Two

*C*LARENCE

S"uicidal idiot!"
"Criminal!"
"You scoundrel!"
The insults came from all directions. But who were these mean-hearted beings? At times I would catch glimpses of hazy faces slipping in and out of the darkness. Then, in despair and with all the strength I could muster, I would rush at them. Frenzied, my blows hit nothing but air. In the end, my anger always came to nothing. Afterwards, I was aware only of their sarcastic laughter as they vanished again into the shadows.

Who could I turn to for help? By then, I was tormented by hunger and thirst. The physical demands of my body, I discovered, continued here as they were on Earth: my beard kept growing; my clothes were beginning to fray and fall apart as the result of my struggles.

The worst part of the trial, though, wasn't being abandoned in this place. It was being surrounded by the sickening forces that poured in from the surrounding darkness. These attacks had unnerved me to the point where I literally couldn't connect one idea to another. I desperately needed to do something—examine the situation carefully, try to understand what was happening, and if I could, reorganize my ideas.

Still, beyond anything I could have imagined, the accusing voices bewildered me:
"What are you looking for, you loser?"
"Where are you going, suicidal fool?"

These accusations, repeated over and over again, utterly dumb-founded me. I might be a fool—but I certainly hadn't committed sui-cide. I had put up a tenacious struggle for life. I could almost hear the doctor at the hospital announcing his last diagnosis, and see the nurses tending to me and changing my dressings during the days that followed my intestinal operation. Indeed, those days were so impressed on my memory that I could still feel the touch of the ther-mometer and the prick of the hypodermic needle. Then, there was the last memory of all: my wife and three children looking at me, shaken by the fear of eternal separation. Then, later, my waking up in that damp and depressing place, where my nightmarish, never-ending flight began.

Why was I being accused of having committed suicide when I had been forced to give up my dreams, my family, and everything I loved? What was going on?

I couldn't figure it out, and I was losing the will to try.

Even the strongest person sooner or later loses the power of resis-tance. So it was with me. Gradually, long bouts of depression replaced my initial firmness and resolution. Despair at the thought of not knowing what would happen to me sapped my former strength. More and more my eyes were full of tears.

But who or what was there to appeal to? The sophisticated intel-lectuality I had brought with me from Earth was of no use to me now. Before the Infinite my knowledge was meaningless—a soap bubble tossed every which way by the winds of transformation. I was a speck carried far in the winds of truth. Yet my essential self continued intact. It occurred to me at one point that I might actually have gone insane and wasn't dead at all. Yet I didn't feel any differ-ent. My conscience was alert and I was, emotionally and intellectu-ally, the same as before. My physical needs continued. I was aware especially of the hunger gnawing at my body's every fiber. Yet, despite the growing weakness, I'd never come close to the point of absolute exhaustion. It helped that now and then I would come across what seemed like wild herbs growing along mere trickles of water. I ate and drank avidly then, but stopped only a few seconds at a time, spurred as I was to keep moving by forces I had no power to resist. Often I would taste the mud by the roadside and, crying, recall how much food there had been in my old life. Often too I would have to hide myself from the rushing crowds of scary beings—truly a blood-curdling sight—that trampled past me like a pack of hungry animals.

When I was nearly at my wit's end, it began to dawn on me that somewhere a Creator of Life must exist. The thought comforted me. On Earth I had hated anything that had to do with religion; I had been a medical doctor and had prided myself on my faddish scientific skepticism. Now I was proof of the failure of that role; I badly needed spiritual consolation. My old sense of self-importance, once so real to me, was gone. I realized that if I was going to find my way in this new world, I would have to change my mental outlook.

When I felt that my energy had vanished completely and my self-esteem was as low as the mud of the Earth; when I no longer had strength even to lift up my head...I implored God to have pity on me, to help me in my desperate situation. For hours I prayed like a helpless child. The tears ran down my cheeks; my whole being seemed to become one great, anguished cry.

Had God really abandoned me? Wasn't I also a child of God, even if—caught up in my foolishness on Earth—I'd never given a thought to divine things? Why wouldn't God, who watched over the birds of the air and the lilies in the field, forgive me? I soon came to see that understanding the mysterious beauty of prayer sometimes requires a good deal of suffering. Before one can fully appreciate the sweetness of hope, one must often know regret, rejection, humiliation.

The moment I recognized that reality, the thick fog that had surrounded me since my arrival broke up and cleared away.

Then I saw someone—in my mind, a messenger from Heaven—a sweet-looking old man who smiled at me paternally. His skin was remarkably free of wrinkles; the glow of health came from him as it might from a much younger man. Gazing intently into my face with large, clear eyes, he said:

"Courage, my child; God hasn't deserted you."

At these words, tears flooded up from the innermost depths of my being. I tried to thank the old man for his kindness, for the relief he had brought, but I was too weak to manage anything but a question:

"Who—who are you, an angel?"

Once again he smiled and answered cheerily:

"My name is Clarence. But angel? No, there you mistake me; I'm only a friend." Seeing how exhausted I was, he added, "Better keep quiet now and try to rest. You need to build up your strength."

He then signaled to two people I hadn't noticed before. "Let's have some emergency care for our friend here," Clarence instructed as the young men approached.

These two, who seemed to be Clarence's assistants, opened a large white sheet and folded it into a small, improvised stretcher, and onto this they gently lifted me up. For his part, satisfied that everything was ready, Clarence nodded and said, once again in a light-hearted voice, "Very well, let's push on and not waste any time. We have to reach Nosso Lar as quickly as possible."

Chapter Three

A COLLECTIVE PRAYER

*A*s I was carried on the stretcher, like an ordinary wounded person, my eyes could glimpse a far more pleasant landscape extending before me.

We came to a large gate built into a tall, vine-covered wall. Clarence, who carried a staff made of some sort of radiant material, went up to the gate and touched a spot. The gate opened and we entered in silence.

On the other side, everything was bathed in a warm glow. In the distance, light played gracefully like the changing pastel palette of a spring sunset. We had now entered an area of considerable size. Before us, on either side, rose fine buildings, surrounded by colorful, well-tended gardens.

After a while, Clarence gave another signal; the aides stopped, and very carefully lay the stretcher on the ground. Looking up, I saw we had come to the entrance of a large white building that, with its wide entrance and many small windows, looked a great deal like an earthly hospital. Two efficient-looking young men in white smocks appeared at the doorway. Without waiting to be asked, they turned to the task at hand, shifted me from the small stretcher onto a hospital gurney, and helped make me comfortable in it.

"Please take him to the east ward," Clarence called after them. "I'm expected elsewhere at the moment, but I'll be around to see him first thing in the morning."

As I was being taken away, I gave the generous old man a smile of thanks. A moment later, we came to a large, pleasant, richly furnished room. My attendants wheeled me into it carefully, and placed me in a comfortable bed.

I felt as full of gratitude toward the two as I had toward Clarence himself, and tried to say something to that effect. But again, I only had enough strength to manage a question, "Will you tell me, please, what world I've come to? And this light— which star does it come from? It's so bright, so—exhilarating."

The attendant to whom I addressed this question spoke to me as if I were an old friend. He stroked my forehead gently.

"We're located in a spiritual sphere close to Earth," he said in a calm voice, "and the sun that's shining on us right now is the same one you always knew. You probably haven't noticed it yet, but visual awareness is much keener here than on Earth, so the sun will appear to be far more beautiful to you than it did before. And soon enough, you'll discover something else: the sun is a source of life, and its light an expression of Our Maker."

The soft light streamed in through my window. Gazing at it, I felt, for the first time, a sense of awe, and allowed myself to sail softly into meditative thoughts. On Earth I had never appreciated the sun, never raised my thoughts to the One who, out of infinite mercy, had given it to us to enlighten our journey. Now I found myself thinking, "Well, I've been blind all this time... and now, after being in the dark for so long, I'm finally seeing the splendor of nature as it really is."

These ideas, much as I hated to give them up, were interrupted by the arrival of nourishment: it consisted of a bowl of broth and a glass of cool water. I had the impression that the water must have been supplemented with some divine substance since only a few sips quickly revived me. The broth, too, probably contained some extraordinary medicine; hard to say if it was a soothing meal, or a strength-building medication. Suddenly I felt much better; a sense of new vigor filled me, and my spirit stirred with emotion. But an even greater surprise was in store.

I had scarcely finished eating when I heard—music. It floated into my room in soft waves of sound rising to higher spheres. The melody went straight to my heart.

"Where is it coming from?" I wondered in amazement, when one of the young attendants noticed my puzzled expression.

"Ah, yes, the music!" he said, smiling. "It's part of the collective prayer service in Nosso Lar. Every department in this service colony is dedicated to Christ, and all our prayers are coordinated with those at the Government Building. I'm going there now. Try to get a little rest, won't you, and I'll be back as soon as the service is over."

As the music filled the air, I could see that he was getting ready to leave. The melody engulfed the room, and I felt a delicate wave of emotions rush through me. I was suddenly overcome by a feeling of joyous anticipation.

"Look, would you mind if I went with you?" I pleaded.

"You're still a bit weak, from the look of you," he said, "but if you feel you can ..."

I don't know what I really expected, but despite the renewing effect of the food and music, I could hardly get out of bed. The young attendant raised me up, though, and I stood upright for the first time in a long while. I grasped the attendant's arm and signaled my readiness to go. He helped me along, step by faltering step, and together in this fashion we reached an enormous hall.

Inside, a great assembly was in deep, silent concentration. The hall itself was sparkling with color. Overhead, delicate garlands of flowers hung from the building's brilliantly lit dome—forming, it struck me even then, a symbol of advanced spirituality. I could hardly contain my astonishment at these sights. Luckily, no one noticed me—they seemed to be waiting for something to happen; so, for the time being, I held in check the questions that were forming in my mind.

In the back of the hall, an intense light reflected brightly from the surface of a gigantic screen. A moment later, it projected into the hall the image of a marvelous temple. Inside the temple sat a venerable old man, immersed in prayer. He was dressed all in white, and around his head shone a halo of brilliant light. Slightly below him stood seventy-two individuals, and they too were deep in silent contemplation, as if attuned with the old man. Among them, I was surprised to see Clarence.

I couldn't restrain my curiosity any longer.

I pulled at the young attendant's arm. He turned and answered in a whisper so soft his words might have been the murmuring of a light breeze:

"Keep still now, please. All the residences and institutions of Nosso Lar are praying with the Governor. If you like, join us in praising the invisible heart of heaven."

No sooner had he stopped speaking than the seventy-two individuals began to sing an exquisite hymn. Clarence's face, among all the other devoted members, seemed bathed in a loftier radiance. The voices rose in thanksgiving, heavenly in their cadences, and in response, vibrations of peace and joy, mysterious to someone like me, floated throughout the hall. Then, as the last notes of the hymn died away, the shape of a wonderful heart, light blue in color and emitting delicate rays of gold, appeared above us in the distance. Soft music arose, it seemed, from very distant spheres. Suddenly, as if from nowhere, beautiful blue flowers began showering down on us. I could see them fall; I tried, in my ignorance, to grasp one or two, without success. The petals touched our foreheads, hovered an instant, and then vanished. Suddenly, I felt the contact of a petal. A surge of energy went through me, as if my heart had been magically touched by a powerful balm.

This impressive service was over all too soon. I went back to my room, aided again by the attentive attendant. Now I was no longer the ailing patient I had been only a few hours before. The first collective prayer I had attended in Nosso Lar had worked a radical change in me. Unexpectedly, and for the first time in many years of suffering, peace touched my soul. After endless years of pain, my wretched heart, troubled and wounded and dry as a wasted goblet, was filled with the sparkling wine of hope.

Chapter Four

Chapter Four

THE DOCTOR

I awoke the next morning having slept a deep and refreshing sleep. Light poured in through my window. It bathed everything in the room in its radiance, and filled my heart with expectation. I felt like a new man, revived in energy and the joy of life. Only one thing was lacking: my home and family. They were painfully far away now.

A number of troubling questions crowded my mind. But for now relief at my rescue and the touching experience in the Assembly Hall aided in calming my spirit, and I didn't spend quite so much time thinking about such things. I was eager to get up and enjoy the beauty of my surroundings. To my disappointment, this would have to be postponed. Without the magnetic cooperation of my attendant, I realized, I wouldn't even be able to get out of bed.

I had barely finished mulling over these thoughts when the door opened and Clarence entered. With him was a stranger—a friendly-looking man, I thought. The two men greeted me cordially, and wished me peace.

Clarence asked about my general health and the attendant, who had stepped in right behind him, quickly filled him in. Clarence nodded in understanding. "This is Dr. Henry de Luna of Nosso Lar's medical staff," he said, introducing his companion.

Dr. de Luna, dressed in the ubiquitous white, radiated good will. He proceeded to examine me in detail. Finally, he stood erect and said, smiling, "Well, it's a pity you've come here by way of suicide."

At these words, Clarence remained unmoved. I, on the other hand, felt a surge of revolt at the idea. Suicide? This was the very same accusation leveled against me by those ghastly beings in that dark place. I was grateful to my rescuers, but this was an accusation I couldn't let pass.

"You are mistaken in that," I said—and my voice betrayed just how aghast I was with the charge. "I fought death for forty days. I suffered through two serious operations because of an intestinal blockage. It was this blockage that caused my death."

"Quite right," the doctor replied in a perfectly composed manner. "But the blockage resulted from very deep causes. Maybe you haven't thought it over enough. The spiritual body carries a detailed history of an individual's habits on Earth."[5]

Very attentively, he pointed out specific parts of my body.

"Now, let's analyze this intestinal area of yours," he said. "The blockage you speak of was actually caused by a malignant tumor—a cancer, in other words. The tumor partially derived from some early indiscretions of yours, in which you contracted syphilis. By itself, the malignancy might not have been so serious if your mental attitudes had been based on principles of tolerance and affability.

"Instead," he went on, "you chose to lead an angry and gloomy life, which attracted destructive vibrations from people around you. Did you ever stop to think that anger attracts negative forces? Your lack of self-control and thoughtlessness in dealing with others, whom you often offended without hesitation, exposed you to the influence of tormented spirits of a lower order. Taken as a whole, these circumstances seriously affected your physical condition.

"My friend," he continued, after a silent and meticulous examina-

----

[5] *Translator's Note: Spiritual body. The spirit is enveloped by a vaporous substance, fine as a mist, which sustains the union between the physical body and the spirit. At death, the spirit sheds the physical body, but preserves the spiritual body. The spiritual body allows the spirit to operate in the denser energy spheres of the physical world. As the spirit advances to more advanced realms the spiritual body will conform to the characteristics of the new environment. Different words have been used to refer to this body: spiritual double, etheric double, astral body, bioplastic body. The Spiritist concept flows from the notion found in Paul's Epistole to the Corinthians: "So will it be with the resurrection of the dead. The body that is sown is perishable, it is raised imperishable; it is sown in dishonor, it is raised in glory; it is sown in weakness, it is raised in power; it is sown a natural body, it is raised a spiritual body. If there is a natural body, there is also a spiritual body." 1 Cor 15:42-44. A more detailed discussion is found in A. Kardec's* The Spirits' Book *(Allan Kardec Educational Society, 1996.)*

tion, "are you aware that both your liver and kidneys were damaged as a result of attitudes that violated the divine gift of life?"

By this time, I was feeling quite uncomfortable. The doctor continued, however, apparently unaware of my distress.

"The body's organs possess superb recuperative powers if employed according to God's purposes. You, my friend, have lost excellent opportunities. The rich task which was entrusted to you by the Higher Spirituality was reduced to a few attempts at a job that was only half done. The intestinal tract was destroyed due to excessive ingestion of food and alcoholic beverages, seemingly unimportant events. In addition, your energies were devoured by the consequences of syphilis. As you can see yourself, the signs of self-destruction are evident."

It was a conclusion that, after some thought, I couldn't disagree with. I started to reflect on the opportunities I had missed. During my life on Earth I had worn many masks, tailoring each one to fit a particular situation. I had never dreamed that one day I would have to account for my behavior during common episodes I once considered meaningless. I had thought that human errors would be taken care of by human law, and that any event not included in those laws would be considered natural and acceptable. I was now faced with a different system designed to verify faults committed: not one in which I was confronted by harsh judges and even harsher verdicts, torture, or the abyss of hell, but in which kind benefactors commented on my weaknesses as one advises an unruly boy away from parental sight. That spontaneous interest, however, was a blow to my human pride. It would have been easier to face my failure, I think, if I had been tormented by demons. Clarence's kindness and sympathy, the doctor's warm tone, the attendant's good-natured patience, all affected me deeply. They turned my pride to shame. I covered my face with my hands in deep sorrow.

Yes, Henry de Luna's conclusions were undeniable. Finally, controlling my impulses of pride, I recognized the extent of my past recklessness—the false notion of personal dignity didn't hold up in the face of justice. Before my spiritual vision there was now a unique, torturing reality: I had in fact committed some form of suicide; I was someone who had squandered the precious gift of the human experience, and was now, an outcast rescued by charity.

Clarence, in his fatherly way, tapped me on the shoulder. "Don't torture yourself, my son," he said gently. "I went searching for you, attending the pleadings of your loved ones, now in higher spheres. Tears now will just cause them grief. Isn't it better to show your gratitude by remaining calm during the examination of your own faults? And let me tell you something: your diagnosis points to unconscious suicide, it's true; but believe me when I say that thousands leave Earth daily in exactly the same way. Now, consider your present state. You've just discovered the treasure of knowledge of your own mistakes: use it well. Regret is a blessing, no matter how late it arrives, but remember that despair won't solve your problems. Put your trust in God and in our brotherly devotion. Your soul is troubled now, so rest it. And consider this: many of us have come here following the same roads you have."

These were generous words—so much so that, like a child, I put my head on his shoulder and my tears escaped freely.

Chapter Five

*U*NDERGOING TREATMENT

"*A*re you Clarence's ward?"

"Yes, that's right."

My questioner, an amiable young man, entered the room smiling.

"I'm Lisias" he informed me. "My attending physician is Dr. Henry de Luna; he visited you yesterday. He has put you under my care until your treatment here is finished."

"You're a nurse, then?"

"A visiting health aide."

"Which means?"

"Oh, a number of things. I help with the nursing, go on rounds, alert doctors if they're needed, help with new patients..."

"I hope there's more than one of you."

"Oh yes, I'm only one of many. Of course, you aren't really aware yet of just how extensive our activities are. For instance, there are over one thousand patients in this ward alone, and this is one of the smallest buildings in our hospital."

"A thousand patients! That's amazing ..."

I was about to begin praising Nosso Lar's medical facilities when Lisias rose quickly from his chair and began examining me. I took the hint and said no more.

"Your intestinal region shows serious lesions," he said, as if confirming information he had already received. "Yes, unmistakable characteristics of cancer. Your liver has several small ruptures, and you have signs of premature kidney failure." Kindly, he turned to me and asked: "Do you know what all of this means?"

I looked away from him for a moment but, remembering

Clarence's advice to remain calm, turned back and said quietly, "Yes, the doctor explained it to me yesterday. These disturbances are all of my own doing ..."

He saw immediately that the topic was a touchy one for me, and covered it over quickly. "I have eighty patients in my care, and of that group fifty-seven are in the same condition as you. And there are many I could show you in worse condition. Some patients arrive disfigured... if they've misused their sight on Earth, they'll come here with their eyes impaired. If they've used their health and athletic abilities to more easily commit crimes, they may show up here with crippled legs or paralyzed. And then there are the ones who return totally insane—they usually lived sexually promiscuous lives and never realized the consequences of their looseness.

"The truth of the matter is that Nosso Lar isn't exactly a settlement of triumphant spirits—at least not in the ordinary sense of the word," he concluded. "The happiness you see around you comes from a single source: the colony's inhabitants have constructive work to do. God has given us an opportunity to serve, and serving fills us with joy."

He paused briefly.

"Please go on with your explanation, Lisias," I said. "Hearing about Nosso Lar makes me feel peaceful and relieved. Isn't it really a home for God's chosen ones?"

In response, Lisias laughed. "Well, let's say we keep in mind that other old teaching: Many are called but few are chosen."[6]

He gazed out of the window, and into the horizon beyond. Some memory from his own past appeared to have caught hold of him suddenly.

"On Earth, a good many religions invite us to the Heavenly Feast," he said, slowly. "And while it's true that those of us who have felt it will never deny God's existence, most of us never answer God's call. We accept a different invitation. We waste our opportunities, wandering away from our right path and letting our whims rule our lives and destroy our bodies. And what is the result? Thousands of us leave the world in a state of total confusion. Do you know that millions of individuals—insane, diseased, ignorant — wander, just as

----

6 *Translator's Note: Matthew 22:14, "For many are called, but few are chosen."*

you did, in the spheres that surround Earth?"

A look of recognition and astonishment must have crossed my face. "Is it really possible?" I said, as much to myself as to Lisias.

"Did you think physical death by itself brings us to a miraculous place?" he returned, seeing my reaction. "Let me tell you that before we get to such a place we need to grow spiritually. Growth of this kind doesn't just come by itself; it requires hard work and devoted service. Even then, despite all our progress, we may have to go back to Earth if we have any wrongs to correct. We are the only ones who can break the chains of hatred that we cast, and replace them with bonds of love. To put it another way, if we've sowed thorns in our own field it wouldn't be fair to ask anyone else to clear it. That's what I mean by "many are called but few are chosen." God doesn't forget anyone, but few of us remember Him."

Here, once again, the idea of individual responsibility faced me. A host of my own faults and weaknesses came crowding in on me. I was on the verge of cursing my own foolishness when Lisias, reading my thoughts, signaled me to stop.

"It won't do any good to accuse yourself," he said, patting me on the shoulder. "If you're really sorry for what you've done, the best course is not to dwell on it and start over again. Right now, let's concentrate on the work we have to do."

He then began a magnetic, healing treatment concentrated mainly on my intestinal area.[7]

"These cancerous areas need special treatment," Lisias explained. "It's what we'll do today. But let me tell you something you shouldn't overlook: all honest work in the field of medicine is based on loving care—but the actual healing is left to the patient. Oh, don't worry, you'll be given the best of treatment, and soon enough you'll

----

[7] *Translator's Note: Lisias' treatment involves placing his hands over Andy's abdominal area to provide a flux of beneficial energies into that region. In serious Spiritist Centers all around the globe, such treatment is often carried out by targeting the seven main energetic regions, or "chakras," of the human body. Reestablishing the equilibrium of such regions occurs by way of an energy flow transmitted from the spiritual world to the patient, or receiver, through the healer. "Just as a blood transfusion represents a renewal of physical forces, magnetic treatment through (bio) energy therapy is a transfusion of spiritual energies, with the distinction that organic resources are obtained from a limited reservoir, while spiritual elements come from an unlimited source". F. C. Xavier in "O Consolador", FEB, chapter 5, question 98.*

start feeling like you're seventeen again. You'll work hard and I have no doubt you'll become one of the best workers in Nosso Lar. But the causes of your illness will remain with you until you neutralize them yourself. The disease germs you nurtured with your lax living and zest for physical indulgence must disappear. Always remember: the body is an instrument. It's given to us so we can cure our souls, if we work at it. That's why we are so wrong when we abuse it."

An instrument to cure our souls. Those words entered the depths of my consciousness. "What endless mercy God shows us," I thought, and the idea moved me to tears.

Lisias, in his relaxed way, finished the day's treatment. Looking up, he saw that I was crying and said, trying to comfort me:

"That's okay, cry if you want to; it's a release, a relief. Tears are a cleansing medicine, if they aren't caused by the wrong feelings such as hatred and anger. I'm leaving now, but I want to say one last thing that might help you. Every day we ought to bless our physical bodies, especially the microscopic organizations that make them up, the cells. So humble, so precious, sometimes misunderstood but always sublime for the service they render. Without them, we would spend thousands of years locked up in spiritual ignorance. Not a pleasant prospect!"

And with those words he placed his hand gently on my shoulder and left to continue on his rounds.

The next day, after the collective prayer, Clarence came by to see me. My attendant was with him.

Chapter Six

*S*OME VALUABLE ADVICE

"*H*ow are you feeling today? A little better, I hope?" my bene-
factor asked, beaming at me with warm generosity.

As patients on Earth often do when they find themselves the center of attention, I let self-pity take command of me. Abusing people's
empathy was an old habit of mine. As the two took seats near me, I
started.

"Yes, sir, I do feel a little better, thank you. But my abdomen hurts
a good deal, and there's this heavy feeling around my heart. To tell
the truth, I'm surprised that I've stood up under all this suffering.
My cross has been heavy. When I think back on it all now, my suffering in that awful place totally sapped my strength."

Clarence listened attentively to my complaints. He even seemed
to be interested. It was an attitude that encouraged me all the more.

"And then, of course," I added, "my soul aches beyond words. The
outside storm is over, thanks to you—but the inner storm!—it keeps
battering away at me. I can't help wondering what has become of
my wife and children, and whether my son—he's the oldest—is still
following the plans I made for him. And what about my daughters?
And especially Celia, my wife? She used to say the loneliness would
kill her if we ever had to leave each other....Where is she, for God's
sake? Is she crying over me?—I can still remember her tears on the
night I died. Or is she dying herself?

"I only wish I knew how long this nightmarish separation has
been going on. I don't have any sense of time anymore. My suffering is unbearable. Unless you are a family man you don't know:
things couldn't be any worse. But I don't think anyone has ever gone

through what I have. I suffered on Earth for years—always struggling, battling diseases, needing things, always being disappointed. And what did I get for it all: a few measly hours of happiness, if that. And then, there was the way I died. First, all the pain and sickness, and then the torture to my spirit.

"Well, what can a person say? Life is just one misery after another, isn't it? I would love to be optimistic, like all the people here. But how can I when there doesn't seem to be any way of gaining peace, and the grief just goes on and on? Life can be a terrible fate, sir."

By this time I had worked myself up into such a state of self-pity that I started to sob.

For his part, Clarence rose quietly from his chair and asked simply:

"My friend, are you seriously interested in being cured?"

"More than anything," I returned.

"Then you must learn not to talk so much about yourself. And particularly not about your sufferings. Self-pity, I must tell you, is a symptom of mental illness, and curing it can be both time-consuming and difficult. Essentially, you are allowing yourself to indulge in negative thought patterns. Those patterns must change, and you must learn to control what you say. And don't think this change can't happen. The only way to gain spiritual balance is to open your heart to the Divine Light. If you think that that is too hard for you, and you see the struggle for redemption as an unfair requirement— well, most unfortunately, you are showing signs of real spiritual blindness. The more your mind dwells on these unpleasant experiences, the more you are their prisoner.

"As for your family, do you think that God, Who shelters and watches over you, wouldn't do the same for your wife and children? Even there, you need some perspective. The family is a sacred institution, true. But keep in mind that it's just one small branch of the universal family, which in its entirety is under God's loving guidance.

"Now, rest assured: you can count on us to help solve your present problems and sketch plans for your future. But none of us have time to spare for long complaints. There is simply too much to be done. In this colony, we undertake the harshest responsibilities as opportunities for our spirits to ascend, remembering, as we plod along under the weight of our debts, that Divine love is unsurpass-

able. If you wish to become one of us, you have to learn to think
properly."

By this time my tears had dried. Clarence's words, delivered in his
usual measured way, had brought me back to my senses, leaving me
ashamed of my weakness. From now on, I promised myself, I would
adopt a different attitude.

But Clarence in his illuminated wisdom wasn't finished. "In your
incarnate life," he continued, "didn't you compete with others for
the best paying positions, knowing how advantageous they were?
Didn't you value those positions as a proper and just means for giving your loved ones what they needed, and adding to their comfort
and stability? Well, the program is much the same here. Only the
perspective is different. On Earth, social convention and money rule
the day. Our work here is aimed not toward the body but the immortal spirit, and its benefits are not for a day but everlasting. The way
we see it, the struggle enriches the soul; toiling to improve yourself
represents a step toward the divine goal. Do you see the difference?
Weak individuals balk at the idea of service. They remain passive,
inactive. Given the choice, they would rather spend their time complaining to anyone who will listen. Strong individuals are a very different breed. They accept the work they're given because they know
it's a constructive step on their path to perfection.

"Please don't misunderstand me. No one blames you for missing
your family—quite the contrary; no one would ever think of taking
away the source of your best and noblest feelings. But tears don't
help the situation in the least. If you indeed love your family on
Earth, it's necessary to accept your present condition here cheerfully and demonstrate good will in order to make yourself useful to
them."

A long pause followed. As Clarence was speaking, I had begun to
see the wisdom of his advice; and now, as I reflected on it, something
stirred in me that was positive and refreshing.

I was still caught up in all these new ideas when Clarence tried
again, "How are you feeling now? A little better?"

These were generous words. We had started all over. Like a father
with the wayward child he loves, Clarence had come back to the old
lesson with the same patience and composure with which he began
it. And I, pleased as a small boy who has been forgiven and is anx-

ious to learn, answered:

"Yes, I'm much better now. And I understand the Divine Will much better, too."

Chapter Seven

ᴌISIAS EXPLAINS

𝓘n the days following, Lisias came regularly to give me treatments, and Clarence visited often.

As I came to adapt better to my new situation, I began to feel more at ease. The pain eased and the strength of movement slowly returned. I noticed, though, that any time I started to think about my problems, I would quickly slip back into my old frame of mind. Despair, fear of the unknown, feelings of alienation would all return. Yet, in spite of everything, I felt a certain inner stability.

One of my greatest pleasures during these days was to lean out of my window and gaze beyond at the great expanse of the horizon. The difference between my surroundings here and those on Earth impressed me enormously. Nearly everything about Nosso Lar and its environs seemed to be an improved version of Earth: the colors were livelier and blended into each other more agreeably; the very substance of things seemed subtler, more delicate. Great trees, full orchards, beautiful gardens spread out everywhere; the ground itself was richer in the variety of its greens. Beyond the plain on which Nosso Lar was situated stood a range of hills, their summits light-crowned. Within the city, graceful buildings rose up at regular intervals, all diverse in their architectural styles, and each with entrances decorated by a wealth of flowers. Scattered among them, I noticed, were charming little bungalows with ivy-covered walls of changing greens and surrounded by multicolored roses. The skies were full of birds, brilliant in their plumage, perching from time to time on the tall white steeples of the buildings. Like gigantic lilies, they seemed to seek out the fringes of heaven. Some distance away,

I also saw, to my surprise, domestic animals moving and grazing beneath the trees. In my introspective quests, I couldn't but be over-whelmed by a flood of questions. I could not comprehend the simi-larities with the forms of Earth; after all, wasn't I in a spiritual dimen-sion? Just as my attendant had told me, the visual sense was more acute here.

One day I asked Lisias, who always had an answer ready for my questions, how it was that a spiritual plane such as this one looked so much like Earth. He didn't disappoint me.

"Death isn't the gate to miraculous change." he said. "We are engaged in a gradual evolutionary process, advancing one step at a time. There is a myriad of planes for those freed from matter, as there are rich and varied conditions for those living on Earth. All souls, all feelings, forms and things, you see, are governed by the same prin-ciples of natural evolution and hierarchy."

"One thing I don't really understand, though, and it worries me a little," I said. "I've been under treatment here for weeks and not one single person that I knew on Earth has come to visit me. I couldn't be the only person in my circle of friends and relatives to learn about the mysteries of death. My parents died before I did, and so did some of my friends. So why haven't they come to see me? Even if only briefly, it would really be a comfort."

I could not contain myself anymore and asked him very directly, "Lisias, do you think we can meet here those who preceded us in the death journey?"

"You think you've been forgotten, then, do you?" he said good-naturedly but with real warmth in his voice.

"Yes, I do, as a matter of fact," I replied. "For instance, my mother used to be devoted to me, and I always relied on her. But I haven't heard a word from her since I've been here, or from my father, either—and he died three years before I did."

"Well, you're flat-out wrong about your mother," Lisias said. "She has been helping you night and day from the time of your last crisis, the one that brought you here. And during that time, she was with you around the clock. You aren't aware yet, are you, that you spent over eight years in the Lower Zone? In all that time she never lost hope. She came to Nosso Lar constantly to intercede for you. She was the one who enlisted Clarence's services, and of course he began visiting you every single day until you, the high and mighty medical doctor, remembered that you were also a child of God. Do you see now?"

My eyes filled with tears. I had no idea that I had been away from Earth so long. I wanted to say something, to find out more about my mother's efforts, but my vocal chords went numb and my heart was too full for words.

"On that day in the Lower Zone," Lisias continued, "when you prayed with your whole heart and came to realize that everything in the universe belongs to God, even your tears were different from what they had been. Tears are like rain in a way: sometimes they are destructive, but they can also be providential. Of course God doesn't wait for our prayers to love us; we must, however, be in a receptive frame to grasp the magnitude of divine love. It's as if we were dirty mirrors and couldn't reflect light. In the same way, God doesn't need our repentance, but you must agree that repentance is good for us. Do you see? When Clarence answered your mother's call for help, he had no trouble finding you at all—you were the one who took your time to find Clarence. And when your mother heard that you had broken through your inner shadows and into the light through prayer, I'm told she cried with joy...."

"Where is she now?" I asked eagerly. "If it's possible, I'd love to see her and hug her, and kneel at her feet!"

"She doesn't live in Nosso Lar but in one of the higher spheres," he told me. "She works there — not just for you, but for lots of others."

He saw that I was disappointed and added:

"Oh, she will be here to see you—don't worry. When you sincerely want something, you're already half way to achieving it. Look at yourself, for example. For years you stumbled along: afraid, distressed, disillusioned. But as soon as you felt the need for the Divine, you expanded your spiritual range, opened yourself to a new vision, and received the aid you needed."

This explanation encouraged me considerably and I said with enthusiasm, "Well then, I wish her to come with all my heart. And so she will!"

Lisias laughed, his face quick and benevolent. "Right you are," he said, preparing to leave. "But consider this: any worthwhile wish must have three components: an active will, effort, and your own worth. In other words, first you have to wish, then work hard toward that wish, and finally deserve to receive what you wish for."

He left me, then, deep in thought and wondering how such an imposing program could have been expressed in so few words.

Chapter Eight

$\mathcal{A}$DMINISTRATIVE ORGANIZATION

$\mathcal{A}$fter several weeks of intensive treatment, I went outside for the first time in the company of Lisias. The streets of Nosso Lar were an impressive sight: wide avenues, bordered by shade-covered side-streets, stretched out before us. The air was clear, and a great spiritual tranquility settled over everything. At the same time, the streets were busy and the place was a hive of activity. Passersby moved by us purposefully, some absorbed in thought; others acknowledging us with nods and smiles.

I was a bit surprised by it all. As usual, Lisias came to my rescue.

"We're now in the district that houses the Ministry of Assistance," he said. "Everything you see here, all of the buildings and houses, are either institutions where the work of the jurisdiction is carried out, or homes for our instructors and staff."

"What kind of work goes on?"I asked.

"Assisting patients, hearing and prioritizing prayers, planning reincarnations on Earth, forming rescue groups for spirits suffering in the lower spiritual zones or on the planet... to put it briefly, the workers here examine problems related to human suffering and work on solutions to them."

"A Ministry of Assistance in Nosso Lar?"

"Why not? Our activities here are guided by an organization. The organization itself is administered by higher spirits who are constantly improving on it. Do you remember the seventy-two assistants who surrounded the Governor at our collective prayers? They are the Ministers of Nosso Lar."[8]

"What sort of work do they administer?"

"There are six Ministries—Renewal, Assistance, Communication, Education, Elevation, and Divine Union. Each one is under the direction of a board of twelve Ministers. The first four Ministries connect us with the Earth; the other two link us to the higher spheres, since our spiritual community is itself a transition zone. The Ministry of Renewal is the one most closely associated with material matters; the Ministry of Divine Union is the most directly connected with spiritual matters. Our instructor Clarence is one of the Ministers of Assistance."

"Amazing," I said when he paused, more impressed than ever. "Who could have imagined finding an organization this complex in the afterlife?"

"You have to remember that the veil of illusion is pretty dense on incarnate spheres," continued Lisias. "The average person on Earth doesn't know, for instance, that every major initiative to improve the order of life on Earth is inspired from higher spiritual planes. Try to think of it like this: if you cultivate the wilderness, you turn it into a garden; if you inspire an undeveloped mind, you turn it into a creative force. Every worthy organization on the material plane has its seed idea in higher spheres."

"And does Nosso Lar have a history like cities on Earth?"

"Of course. Near-Earth institutions all have their own particular nature and history. Nosso Lar is an old settlement. A group of distinguished Portuguese pioneers founded it in the sixteenth century. After death, they chose to settle in the spiritual planes over Brazil. According to colony records, they struggled mightly at first, just as settlers would on Earth. There were huge areas largely untouched in these planes, very much like Earth's uncultivated and inhospitable regions.

"It was hard and discouraging work even for the strongest ones... and they had cause for discouragement. Around us now we see fine buildings and feel the delicate mental vibrations of the city. But in those days the place was pretty rough and occupied by the spirits of

----

8 *Translator's Note: The designation of Minister in Nosso Lar does not carry any religious association, it is rather an administrative title. The organization structure of Nosso Lar, head by a team of Ministers, reporting to a Governor, is particular to this institution. The forms of organization and the titles of their administrators must be as varied there, as they are on Earth.*

the region's indigenous people. Their intellects were primitive and
their mental organization elementary. Luckily, the pioneers didn't
lose heart. They went about their work and followed the example of
the Old World settlers on Earth—except that instead of violence, war,
and slavery, they built through perseverance, brotherhood, and spiritual love."

Soon, we came to a large square. It had been designed with considerable artistry, and was filled with beautiful gardens. At its center
rose a magnificent palace, crowned with a series of towers so tall
they disappeared from sight.

"That's the Government Building," Lisias explained. "It's where
the founders placed the corner-stone of the colony, and where the
six Ministries I told you about come together. You can see the main
streets on which the Ministries are located leading away from it. The
Ministries actually start in the Government Building, and from there
they fan out in a triangle. This is also where the Governor lives, by
the way. The central administration has a staff of three thousand;
but, believe me, the Governor is the most tireless and dedicated
worker in the whole community. The other Ministers sometimes
travel to other spheres to renew energies and gain new knowledge—and the rest of us have our amusements, too. But the
Governor has no leisure time whatsoever. He requires all of us to
take vacations periodically and rest up; he never takes one himself.
He works constantly. He finds his strength in never-ending service,
you might say. I have been here for forty years, and, except for the
collective prayers, I have never once seen him at a social function.
But his mind radiates power, and it reaches into every branch of
activity here. His loving assistance is felt by everyone, and everywhere, in the community."

He paused for a while, evidently lost in his admiration of the
Governor. Finally he said, "Just a while ago, we celebrated the one
hundred and fourteenth anniversary of his administration."

He interrupted his explanation then, and we walked on together
for a while reverently and silently. Meanwhile, I took the time to
gaze in wonder at the great towers of the Government Building,
some of them rising so high they seemed to touch the sky itself.

Chapter Nine

THE PROBLEM OF NUTRITION[9]

I mpressed as I was by the sight of the gardens, I was also growing tired at this stage of our walk.

"Do you mind if we sit down on one of those benches over there?" I asked.

"Not at all," Lisias replied. We sat down, stretched, and looked around us. A soothing calmness enveloped my whole being. Nearby a spring projected colored streams in the air creating a gracious ballet of shifting silhouettes. The sight of this complex set of gardens and buildings brought to my mind a question I had intended to bring up to my companion.

"The Colony here is so huge," I said. "I can't help thinking of all the problems that must come up in running it. For instance, the problem of supply. There isn't a Ministry of Economy, is there?"

"Not any more," replied Lisias. "The fact is that economic issues used to be a good deal more important than they are now. That was before our Governor decided to cut down, as much as he could, on practices that reminded us of the purely physical world. Part of his

----

[9] *Translator's Note: The concept of nutrition in the spiritual realm has little relation to Earth's. Indeed, use of the word reflects the limitations of our vocabulary. The author seeks to describe the process utilizing words that convey the notion of energy replenishment in its general form. The reference to substances in the form of juices, liquids, or broth is part of a set of images that make sense to us. Neither the spirit nor the spiritual body has a digestive or sympathetic system. Moreover, this process of energy replenishment is limited to the lower spheres of the spiritual realm. It must also be kept in mind that Nosso Lar is a transitional organization where the majority of the individuals are still struggling with their spirituality, and are been treated and prepared for a new reincarnation. More advanced processes are explained in later chapters.*

plan was to put the Department of Supply, as it was called, directly
under the control of the Central Administration and turn it into a
simple distribution office.

"That turned out to be a very beneficial decision. Our records
show that a century ago the colony went to great lengths to introduce its citizens to the principle of simplicity. Not a universally
popular idea, as you've guessed. Many of the newcomers to the
Colony were very attached to their earthly vices. They insisted on
elaborate food and fine drinks, abuses that caused trouble everywhere except for Divine Union, which has nothing to do with
physical concerns. Almost every department had its share of difficulties. The Governor did everything he could to bring this situation to an end; and the moment he took on his administrative
duties at Nosso Lar, he introduced a number of decisive measures
against it.

"Some of our older workers told me about what happened.
According to them, the Governor asked for two hundred instructors from a very high plane. The instructors were charged with
teaching the colony´s citizens about breathing techniques and the
absorption of life-sustaining elements from the atmosphere. They
went around giving lectures on the subject. But many of our own
'experts' were against the idea. According to their way of thinking,
since we are a transition colony, it was unfair and even dangerous
to submit newly arrived individuals to such drastic changes. Those
changes, they argued, would seriously damage our patients' spiritual bodies. But the Governor wouldn't give in.

"For thirty straight years, the instructors gave lectures, provided illustrative examples, went into technical explanations (pretty
simplified for us, no doubt). But not everyone could be brought
into the fold. A number of the more vocal individuals even went
so far as to organize public demonstrations against the Governor's
actions. More than ten times the Ministry of Assistance was over-
burdened with patients with ailments that they, the patients,
attributed to the deficiencies of the new diet. Often these occur-
rences were followed by a rise in the noise level of those who
combated the measure. Though it would have been within the
rights of the Governor to punish his critics, he never did. Instead,
he invited them to the Government Building and explained to

them, in a peaceful way, all the aims and benefits of the new program. He offered regular talks on its superiority as a means of spiritualizing the whole colony; and for more stubborn ones he even arranged study trips to the higher planes. An unusual step, but it convinced a lot of them."

"How did the situation end?"

"The Governor held out for twenty-one years, and finally the Ministry of Elevation gave in and cut its supplies to necessities only. The Ministry of Education, which was filled with individuals whose primary focus was on the mathematical sciences, didn't come around until later. They were, in a literal sense, statisticians, still caught up in calorie and protein requirements—very important for physical bodies, as you're aware, but not relevant to our bodies here. Anyway, the individuals at Education became the new system's most vigorous opponents. Every week they sent the Governor long reports. These reports showed him the results of tests, threw lots of graphs and numbers at him, and in general warned him not to continue. They got pretty sure of themselves after a while, but the Governor never lost patience.

"In a matter of this importance, the Governor didn't want to act alone, so he asked for help from spirits of a higher order who guide Nosso Lar by way of the Ministry of Divine Union. Together, they went over all the documents carefully, which of course took some time. In the meantime the scientists at the Ministry of Education were coming up with new arguments every day. The government proceeded cautiously; but a crisis in the Department of Renewal, now called the Ministry of Renewal, was quickly developing. Some of the less developed individuals there started getting caught up in Education's rebellion and pushing their resistance activities even further. Soon Nosso Lar was filled with an atmosphere of unrest that divided the city and opened it up to offensives by disturbed entities from the Lower Zone. That is exactly what happened. Hostile spirits tried to infiltrate Nosso Lar, taking advantage of the service lapses in the Department of Renewal where a good many of the workers were bending the rules, bringing in supplies from the outside in order to feed their own addictions.

"Well, the alarm went up. This was an obvious threat to all of us.

The Governor, though, never lost his composure. He asked the Ministry of Divine Union for a meeting and, after coordinating his actions with our highest counsel, he temporarily shut down the Ministry of Communication. Next he ordered the cell-blocks under the building which houses the Department of Renewal prepared for solitary confinement of the most stubborn rebels. He also issued a warning to the Minister of Education, whose high-handedness he had withstood for thirty years, and ordered the suspension of any assistance whatsoever to the Lower Zone until further notice. Then, for the first time in his administration, he had the city walls rigged up electrically. Anyway, the colony never waged a battle. It was, on the government side, a defensive posture. But it was a determined defense. The crisis lasted for over six months. During that time the diet of Nosso Lar was reduced to life-supporting elements in the air, and the electrical, magnetic, and solar energies in the water. The colony also felt, for the first time, what the displeasure of a just and kind individual really meant. Finally the crisis ended in a complete government victory."

"How were the problems with the different Ministries resolved?" I asked.

"The Ministry of Education finally admitted its mistakes and even took part in the readjustment work that followed. Nosso Lar's citizens were overjoyed and held public celebrations. At one point the Governor was moved to tears by their expressions of gratitude. Good understanding between him and the city's citizens, he said, was his greatest reward in life.

"Finally, the Department of Renewal was promoted to Ministry status, and the city went back to its usual routine. Since then the Ministries of Renewal and Assistance have been allowed to store supplies of denser food substances because the spiritual level of many of their patients is so low. But in all the other Ministries, the diet is limited strictly to essentials, according to the laws of good spiritual health. Nowadays, you'll be interested to know, everyone agrees that the Governor was right and that what looked like an arbitrary act of power on his part was really intended to help our spiritual ascent. In fact, with the reduction in our dependence on material things, our attention to spirituality has increased enormously."

"A remarkable story," I said. At this point, Lisias grew silent, leaving me to meditate on the great lesson he had just given me.

Chapter Ten

𝒯HE WATER PARK

𝑀y growing interest in nutrition one day prompted Lisias to invite me to go on a field trip with him.

"Let's go take a look at the colony's reservoir," he said. "It's huge and quite a sight. Besides, you'll get a chance to see some things that'll interest you and learn a little about the essential importance of water in a transition colony."

"Sounds terrific," I replied, "you've aroused my curiosity. When do we go?"

"How about right now?"

Half an hour later we had arrived at the corner of the public square.

"Here's where we wait for transportation," he told me.

"Transportation?"

At just about that time a large vehicle, something akin to a bus, approached the square cruising smoothly a few feet above the ground. It stopped and lowered itself down to our level. This unusual conveyance seemed to be made of a strong but highly flexible material and was of considerable length. From the number of rods on its roof, I guessed that it must have been connected to some wireless energy source (later, on a visit to one of the Traffic and Transportation stations, I confirmed this hypothesis.)

The two of us made our way into the bus, settling down into comfortable, roomy seats. I felt a little uneasy at first, a little self-conscious about the presence of so many unknown passengers.

The vehicle, I soon discovered, was capable of traveling at enormous speeds, making it impossible for anyone so inclined to take in the passing scenery. In any case, despite stopping once in a while to take on and let off passengers, we covered a great deal of ground. About forty minutes later Lisias said, "We're here," and we got off at the next stop.

Before us spread out a woodland scene of superb beauty. The trees were in full bloom, and the fresh air was heavy with the scent of the flowers growing on them, and growing everywhere. It was all a miracle of color and light. Immediately beyond us, a magnificent river wound its leisurely way between green banks that were sprinkled with delicate, blue flowers. Shimmering in the sun, the river's slow-moving waters reflected the varied hues of the sky like a well-polished mirror. We were not, however, in a wilderness. Here and there wide paths had been cut through the woods, all leading in different directions; at regular intervals along them stood great oaks and elms, offering shade to pathwalkers. Nearby, carved into fanciful shapes, were benches that invited one to sit and rest.

"What an extraordinary place!" I said, venting my very real enthusiasm for this new aspect of the colony.

"We call it the Water Park," Lisias told me. "It's one of the finest sections in the whole colony. Lovers like to come out here and exchange vows of love and faithfulness for their future experiences on Earth."

This last comment brought up a world of questions, but Lisias was intent on showing me the Park and talked on, caught up in his own delight in the place. He pointed to a large building in the distance and said:

"That's the colony's water works. The waters of the Blue River—the one you are looking at—are drawn off into canals and from there piped into every district in the colony. The river comes together again on the other side of the colony, beyond the section that belongs to the Ministry of Renewal, and takes up its regular course, headed for the great ocean of cosmic forces—which, incidentally, is undetectable from Earth."

My mind was spinning with new interests, but I held back and said, "Well, it's certainly unlike Earth water".

"As a matter of fact," explained Lisias, "water here has quite a different density than it does on Earth. It's much lighter—purer."

"Which Ministry controls its distribution?"

"Actually, that's one of the rare activities of a material nature that falls under the Ministry of Divine Union."

"Oh? How do you reconcile the two?"

Lisias smiled.

"Very few people on Earth recognize the importance of water, " he said. "Our attitude here in Nosso Lar is different, probably because we know a great deal more about it. Look at it this way, on earth religious schools teach that the Lord created the waters. Thus, it makes sense to think that all this water can be preserved in all it's original purity with a little assistance from us.

"We're very grateful to God and his divine collaborators for this gift, of course, but we understand that energy and attention are required in order for the utmost benefits to be reaped. As I say, we're very well acquainted with the properties of water. We know, for instance, that it is one of the best energy conductors imaginable, no matter what the energy type. We use it here mostly for nutritional and medical purposes. But before that happens, it undergoes special treatment. Over at the Ministry of Assistance you'll find several departments devoted entirely to mixing pure water with certain elements taken from the sun's rays and from spiritual magnetism. In most Colony districts, water prepared like this is the basis of our diet.

"Of all of us, as you know, the Ministers of Divine Union have reached the highest level of spirituality. Because of that, the job of magnetizing the waters of the Blue River has fallen to them. To put it simply, they purify it enough so that it can be used by everyone in Nosso Lar. Later, nutritional and medical components are added— very specialized work—and the water is ready. After it is used it flows back into the Blue River's natural channels, as I've said, carrying some of our spiritual qualities with it."

I was surprised and amazed at what Lisias had told me about the treatment of water here.

"On Earth, I never heard explanations of this sort," I muttered.

"People on Earth don't pay as much attention to their environment as they should," said Lisias. "For centuries the ocean has kept Earth's environment in balance. If only humans could recognize it and not abuse it. Why, the human body itself is mostly water; water gives people their bread, makes their cities thrive, and makes home life possible. People, however, go on acting as if they're the absolute masters of the world, and forget that they're children of God before anything else.

"There will be a time, though, when humans will recognize that the nature of water is divine, and will follow our example and truly value God's gift. They'll also realize that water absorbs the spiritual characteristics of the people in every home it touches. Did you know that? Water doesn't just carry away waste material; it becomes filled with mental vibrations, too."

"Is that what you meant by saying that the Blue River contains some of your spiritual qualities?"

"Absolutely. Water may be noxious in base hands, but healing when in the service of generous minds. Pure water, as it moves, spreads the blessings of life; it carries away human thoughts of bitterness, hatred, and worry. All of this, in addition to its ordinary functions of keeping the body and home clean. And in that way it does the work of Divine Providence."

Lisias stopped speaking and went over to the Blue River, looking at it with reverence. I joined him and looked out over the tranquil waters with a different feeling, for they had roused in my mind lofty thoughts that I wouldn't have imagined myself capable of on Earth.

ℒEARNING ABOUT THE PLANES OF LIFE

"*T*here is nothing I'd like more than to show you around the Colony," Lisias said, "but I have many duties and pressing demands on me right now. But, don't worry, you'll soon have a chance to visit everything. It's just that the Ministries are such vast centers of intense work that a worthwhile tour of any of them would take days. But we can always contact Minister Clarence. He'll be able to fix you up with a permit that'll get you into any department you'd like."

We were back on the vehicle by this time and, full of delight from our experiences, we were on our way home.

I was a little more in control of myself on this return trip: the uneasiness I had felt at first was gone and I didn't feel nearly so self-conscious in the presence of so many passengers. The visit to the Park was stimulating. In fact, I was fairly relaxed, and had soon forgotten my surroundings, letting my mind wander over some of the questions I had—the list of which was growing by yards almost from one minute to the next. At last I turned to Lisias.

"Tell me, are all the spiritual colonies like this one?" I asked. "Do they all have the same characteristics and activities?"

"No, not at all," he replied. "Don't different regions and towns on Earth have features all their own? Well, it's the same here. In fact, here the differences from place to place can be even greater. In some ways we're like Earth: here, for instance, people are grouped depending on their common origins and the goals they're trying to reach. But each colony, just as each individual, stands at different spiritual levels. They're moving toward perfection at their own rates, and so our collective experiences vary. What you see here is only one example of a colony. The first pioneers we talked about earlier drew on the knowledge and experience of workers in other colonies constantly. That kind of exchange has never stopped; there are now spirits forming their own colonies who ask us for advice. But essentially each colony has its own character."

"What about the idea of the division into Ministries? Did that start in Nosso Lar?"

"More or less, yes. Nosso Lar's pioneers visited New Dawn, one of our neighbors and a very important spiritual colony. They studied the organization there and saw how activities were distributed according to departments. The idea impressed them and they adopted it. They did make one basic innovation: they substituted the word 'Ministry' for 'Department'—except in the case of the Ministry of Renewal, which was transformed into a Ministry by our present Governor. This kind of organization seemed to be more spiritually meaningful to our pioneers."

"I can see how that would be true," I said.

"Ah, now you're catching on!" Lisias continued with a broad smile. "In our colony the stress is on hierarchy and order. The only criterion employed for promotion decisions is merit. And, believe me, anyone who's assigned an important position has earned it. In ten years, only four individuals have been promoted to work in the Ministry of Divine Union. As a rule, most of us, after a long period of apprenticeship and service, reincarnate so we can continue working our way to enlightenment."

My mind spun with curiosity, but Lisias continued on excitedly.

"Newcomers who show an interest in cooperating with their treatment are placed with the Ministry of Assistance. The more uncooperative ones go to the Ministry of Renewal. In time they begin to improve, and then they're admitted as helpers in the various services provided by the Assistance, Communication, and Education Ministries. It's a way for them to prepare for future tasks on Earth. A few individuals—only a few—ever get the privilege of long stays in the Ministry of Elevation. And it's very rare for individuals to reach the level of the staff of the Ministry of Divine Union. Let me tell you, the qualifications for positions in Nosso Lar aren't just a matter of having high ideals. We work hard here. We aren't like spirits trapped on the earthly plane—ghosts without any sense of purpose."

"It must take special qualities to work in any of the Ministries," I said with curiosity.

"Oh, yes," he chimed in earnestly, but also with a good-natured tone in his voice. "If you want to see difficult, complex work, visit the Ministries of Assistance and Renewal: you have to be in excellent spiritual condition in both. At Communication, the requirement is a high standard of individual responsibility; Education wants well-trained minds with a solid work ethic. Elevation requires that you demonstrate a capacity for self-denial and show that you have reached a high degree of spiritual awareness. The Ministry of Divine Union asks for great wisdom and real universal love."

"What about the Government?" I said.

"The Government, of course, is the center of all administrative activities and controls a great number of services, too, so you can imagine the kind of detail and efficiency needed there. The individuals in Government take care of all support activities such as nutrition, the distribution of electrical energy, traffic and transportation: in short, everything that's required for day-to-day functioning.

"Individuals work until what needs to be done is finished. There is never any shirking during the course of the day here. On the other hand, rest is important in the Colony. People take periodic breaks from their responsibilities so that the weight of work will remain evenly distributed."

"Equality all around, I see."

"Yes, the one exception is the Governor himself. He works constantly. Even when he could take advantage of rest and relaxation, he works."

"And never leaves the Government Building?"

"Only if the public welfare really requires it. Of course, there is his Sunday visit to the Ministry of Renewal."

"Why there?"

"Because the Renewal district has the biggest number of problematic and disturbed individuals—those still wired to their friends in the Lower Zone. You'll find a huge number of wrongdoing spirits there, too. So on Sundays, after the collective prayers in the Government Building's Great Temple, the Governor spends the

afternoon working with the Ministers of Renewal on the most difficult cases. He sacrifices a lot to help ease the plight of those individuals."

The vehicle finally pulled into our stop near the Hospital. I looked
forward to going back to my room. I was grateful, really, to have it to
come back to.

We were walking in the direction of the Hospital, when I noticed
something about the street I had been aware of before but had
neglected to ask about.

"That music," I said to Lisias, "It seems to be everywhere. And the
melodies are beautiful. Where does it come from?"

"From our workshops," replied Lisias simply. "Some years ago,
the Government conducted a few experiments on the benefits of
music; it tested the effects of different melodies on worker produc-
tivity. Since then, music has been an integral part of all our activities."

By this time we had reached the hospital entrance. We had no
sooner gone through the opening doors, when an attendant
appeared and said, "Lisias, you are needed right away in the west
wing."

Lisias looked at me with a knowing gesture, and hurried on his
way. I went up to my room, my mind exploding with a hundred
ideas and questions.

Chapter Twelve

THE LOWER ZONE

After listening to all of Lisias' s wonderful explanations, I was eager to explore some of the areas we had talked about. His references to spirits in the shadowy Lower Zone had aroused my curiosity especially. Earth's religious instruction is so lax that newcomers to this plane often arrive in a state of confusion about these matters, and I was confronted with a question many have asked before and since: What could the Lower Zone be? I had heard about Hell and Purgatory in the Catholic sermons I had attended (mostly out of a well-developed sense of social obligation), but I had never heard of the Lower Zone before.

The next time I met Lisias I had all my questions prepared beforehand. As always, he listened carefully.

"Well now," he said when I had finished, "you ought to know that region very well. You were there long enough."

The memory of it made me shudder.

"The Lower Zone begins on Earth's crust. It's a shadowy region which harbors those who neglected spiritual realities and the duty they were supposed to perform on Earth—many of them undecisive people, or just those who chose to do wrong."

"What do you mean by `the duty they were supposed to perform'"?

"Ah! when a spirit reincarnates, it promises to carry out a task or mission that furthers God's work. However, when the individual reaches the rough patches of the journey, the promise gets forgotten, and whatever seems to serve him or her better put in its place. Thus, he or she resumes the old habits of cultivating hatreds and loving their close relations exclusively—forgetting that hate isn't justice and passion isn't real love. All excess with no specific beneficial goals leads to an unbalanced life.

"So, after physical death, the spirits that are still caught up in their earthly fixations—always a huge number, I'm sorry to say — stay in the spiritual region closest to the planet."

"But what about those who perform their duties? Don't they get any credit for it?"

"Yes, indeed," Lisias replied. "A duty well done is a gateway; through it we enter the Infinite. It brings us closer toward our goal, and that goal is the sacred union with God. So it's only natural that someone who neglects responsibilities is going to postpone that blessing—indefinitely. "

"Now you've lost me completely."

Lisias gave me a look of sympathy, generously accepting my almost total unawareness of spiritual principles. He thought for a moment and tried again.

"Let's see if an analogy will help," he said. "Suppose each of us returns to Earth wearing filthy clothes, and our one objective in that return is to wash those clothes in the water of human life. The dirty clothes, you understand, represent our spiritual bodies, which were debased in past lives. Now, this new opportunity to clean our dirty clothes is a real blessing, a gift to us. But suppose we forget all about why we came to Earth—which is what happens when we make the change from the spiritual to the physical plane? Instead of cleaning those clothes, something we can only do by positive action, let's say we get them even dirtier than they were before. We've now taken negative action, and as a result we take on even more obligations. We returned to Earth to get rid of all our imperfections, since we understood that they are inconsistent with the higher planes. So can we realistically expect to reach those planes when we're in an even worse condition?

"The Lower Zone is, then, a purification region where the individual slowly purges the residue of mental illusions he or she has overloaded life with. Do you see?"

"It couldn't be clearer," I said, thoroughly convinced.

These explanations, he saw, were of real use to me, and he went on eagerly:

"The Lower Zone ought to interest everyone on Earth because everything that doesn't agree with the purposes of heaven converges right there. Think of the wisdom that Divine Providence demonstrated in permitting the creation of this transitional region near Earth. In the Lower Zone there are hordes of unaware and stubborn spirits that are not evil enough to be shuttled to colonies where expiation is harder, or noble enough to be taken to a higher spiritual plane. In a real way, they are still close to their incarnate friends; and in fact, if certain vibratory laws weren't in effect, the two wouldn't be separated at all. But you can see from this how so many serious disturbances in this region are possible; this shouldn't be any surprise. There's also another cause of disturbance: rebellious spirits of every kind group together. They crowd together based on their common tendencies and desires.

"You know how people on Earth get irritate when the postman doesn't show up or the train is late? Spirits in the Lower Zone are like that. It's full of angry beings. After their deaths, these people are disappointed to find that God isn't going to be there to satisfy their every little need. To their great frustration, in a short time they realize that the crown of glory and spiritual fulfillment is reserved only for those who've served God's plan. At that point they stand revealed for what they really are, and end up giving themselves wholly to low and ruinous endeavors. They form a sort of community. Except that, unlike Nosso Lar, this community is filled with frustrated, lazy, perverted individuals. It's a zone of tyranny and bondage, of the users and the used."

"But these individuals just seem to roam around. Why is that? Don't they have any kind of rules or organization?"

Lisias shook his head. "In order to have organization, you have to be organized yourself. That quality has to be part of your make-up. But the Lower Zone is like a house where there is never any food, and no one has a clue as to what to do about it. Everybody complains, nobody yields to reason. Put it another way—on Earth if you're a traveler not paying attention to the schedule, you're going to miss your train; if you're a farmer and you plant the wrong kind of seed, you're not going to get a crop to harvest. To get these things right, you have to have some capacity for organization.

"The spirits in the Lower Zone don't have that capacity. But please consider this: even in the shadows and through all the trials of the Lower Zone, individuals are always under Divine protection, and each one stays there for exactly the time he or she needs to stay, no more, no less. They are why Nosso Lar exists in the first place. God brings settlements like ours into existence so that we can serve in their deliverance and healing."

"So the Lower Zone is a kind of continuation of the earthly, incarnate plane," I said.

"Absolutely," Lisias returned. "Moreover, it provides the medium for the mind-to-mind communication that is a feature of human life on Earth. This region is populated also with discarnate beings and the millions of thought-forms bred by people everyday. Everyone radiates his or her particular thought patterns, no matter what plane they are on. Here is a fact for you to mull over: whatever else an individual is, he or she is also a nucleus that radiates forces—forces that can create, transform, or destroy. Science doesn't understand the mechanism yet, but these forces—in the form of ideas—are projected as waves. When we think, we create at some level. Thoughts are the way people on Earth communicate with individuals in the Lower Zone who have similar inclinations. Every soul is a powerful magnet. An extensive invisible spirit society exists that coexists at many levels with the visible one."

"I'm beginning to see what the workers in Nosso Lar are up against," I said.

"The toughest missions in the Lower Zone go to the most devoted helpers in the Ministry of Assistance," explained Lisias. "They are like firefighters in cities on Earth. The firefighters' work is exhausting and dangerous because of the flames and smoke they have to face day in and day out. The volunteers to the Lower Zone experience something on the same order. They have to withstand, on a regular basis, enormous surges of distressing energies sent out by thousands of minds engaged in wrong-doing, or enduring excruciating life experiences. Let me tell you, it takes a great deal of courage and a real willingness to sacrifice yourself to help those who still don't understand or refuse the help you're offering them."

This explanation touched me more than any I had heard yet. A response stirred deep within me and I found myself saying, "I would give anything if I could do work like that—help those unfortunate individuals, feed them the bread of understanding."

Lisias gave me a long, penetrating look and said, after thinking about it for a few moments, "A generous thought, but I wonder if you really feel up to such an undertaking yet."

And with those words, more telling than I knew at the time, he took his leave.

Chapter Thirteen

*I*N THE MINISTER'S OFFICE

*G*radually I grew stronger. A new vigor came back into my life—and with it a new problem. With each passing day I began to feel the need for work and activity again. I longed to get back to some occupation that would fill up my hours—to what, on Earth, is called a regular work day.

Earth! When I remembered my work there, it was only to shake my head in disappointment. "You really missed some terrific opportunities," I found myself thinking again and again.

Fifteen years of medical practice and what did I feel?—emptiness of heart. Well, I didn't want that to happen here. But so far I was like a farmer standing out in the middle of a field, fully capable of working and willing to do it but with his hands tied behind his back. I was surrounded at the Hospital by patients, but wasn't allowed to approach them as a friend, doctor, or researcher; I could hear the groans of sufferers coming from rooms adjacent to mine but couldn't lend a hand, not even as a member of the nursing or first-aid staff.

I did, of course, understand the reality behind this state of affairs. On Earth, becoming a licensed physician was a matter of going to medical school and studying the assigned textbooks. In Nosso Lar the requirements were different; so were the treatment methods. Medical practice here started in the heart, and the basic treatment consisted of brotherly care and love. I couldn't offer qualifications of that kind. The lowliest nursing assistant in the place was far more knowledgeable about curing patients than I was. My science didn't count anymore. So, even though I needed an occupation, I suspected that — for the time being anyway — any application for work I might make would just be an intrusion on somebody else's rights.

As usual, when faced with a problem, I turned to Lisias.

"Why don't you ask Clarence?" he suggested. "He's always asking about you, you know, and he'd probably do anything he could to help."

All of a sudden I was filled with a new enthusiasm. So it was that later that afternoon I sought to see the Minister, but was told that he could only see me the next morning in his private office.

I waited for the next day with no small anxiety. The following morning I made my way to his office and, to my surprise, found three people already in the waiting room. He had, I discovered, arrived long before us and, at the moment, was tending to business more important than receiving visitors and petitioners.

When this work was over, the Minister had us shown in, two at a time. This way of conducting a private meeting puzzled me. I later learned that the Minister simply preferred dealing with two individuals at a time. He had found that a particular case might help both the parties involved and serve the common good. And it saved time.

The other visitor in the waiting room was an elderly woman. After several long minutes the Minister invited us to come into his office.

"How are you, my friends?" the Minister said, cheery in his welcome. "How can I help you?" he began, turning to the woman.

"Minister Clarence," she said, "I've come to ask, to beg, that you intercede on behalf of my two sons. I can't stand being separated from them any more! I just can't stand it ! I've learned that their lives on Earth are growing harder and harder, and their trials seem to have no end in sight. It's breaking my heart. Oh, I realize God's plans for them are loving and just. But I'm a mother. I can't stop worrying about them. I can't help grieving."

Having got so far in her petition, she broke into tears. Clarence stared at her with great generosity in his eyes. Compassion was written in his features. His words, however, were delivered in a firm, steady voice.

"But, sister," he told her, "if you agree that God's plans for your sons are holy and just, what can I do?"

"I'd like you to consider ..." her voice trailed off. "Well, I'd—I'd like to be able to protect my sons on Earth myself," she said, finally getting it out.

"My dear," he said after a pause, "in order to guide others, we have to grow in the spirit of humility and service ourselves. What would you think of a father who said, 'There's nothing I want more than to provide for my children, but then stayed home and did nothing? God created the laws of service and cooperation, and one can't break them without facing the consequences. Doesn't your conscience tell you anything on this score? Tell me," he went on, "how many hour-bonuses can you present to support your request?"

The answer came even more hesitantly than before.

"Three hundred and four," she said, finally seizing on the right figure.

"But you have been here for six years," Clarence told her, while keeping out of his tone any hint of the accusatory. "Don't you believe you should have done more for the Colony than that? If I remember correctly, after you recovered from your trials in the Lower Zone, I offered you a fine job in the Ministry of Communications' Vigilance Patrols."

"Oh that!" she interrupted, suddenly quite alert to what was evidently an unpleasant memory. "I couldn't stand it—always fighting with those pitiful beings. I couldn't do it. It just wasn't in my nature."

"Well, what about the place I found for you with the Fellowship of Assistance?" Clarence said. "That was a real chance for redeeming service."

"It was worse than the other one!" she protested again. "All the swearing and the immorality and the filth. That's all I saw there—filthy creatures."

"But I realized that you were having trouble there and reassigned you, didn't I? To the ward for the mentally disturbed. Your cooperation with the staff there would have been a great help."

"And I did my best!" the woman replied. "No one can say any different. But they really scared me, all those raving lunatics. I would have to be a saint to stay there a minute longer than I did."

Clarence, though, wasn't finished. "I don't think you've found my interest in you a very welcome one, sister," he said a little sadly. "You know, when I found another place for you with the Department of Investigation and Research of the Ministry of Education, you simply walked out and withdrew to the Park of Rest".

"That place was unbearable, " she explained. "I couldn't endure the atmosphere there. You have no idea what it's like to be surrounded by all those strange energies, to do exhausting experiments every day, and on top of it all to put up with harsh supervisors."

"My friend," he said, "I think we are well-acquainted enough for me to tell you something important about the Colony here. Helping others requires two qualities: the desire to serve and meekness of heart. If you want to help somebody, here or anywhere, you first have to establish good relations with others—benefactors, friends, aids, whoever you're called on to work with. Now, you want to assist your sons—I understand that. But before you can give them any aid whatsoever, you have to establish an inner atmosphere of empathy with others. Without their cooperation we can do very little. We are not really that different from Earth in this respect. A farmer there plants his crops and works his fields, and he is rewarded by the appreciation of the people who enjoy the harvest. A worker follows the orders of a demanding supervisor to the letter; and as a result, he can feed his family. A worker who is filled with the spirit of cooperation earns his employer's good will, as well as that of his friends and anyone else interested in his work. The same goes for an administrator who can only succeed when he or she learns to serve and follow rules. Do you see that?"

"What you have to keep in mind," Clarence continued, "is that all service that's useful to others belongs to the Universal Giver."

"Tell me now," he said, "what you would do on Earth if you haven't learned to withstand the hardships that you encounter here? Oh, I don't doubt for a moment that you're concerned about your sons. I know you're devoted to them. But you would be handicapped there and wouldn't be able to do a thing for them, as hard as you tried."

"I know you want to help," he said. "But to attain the joy of helping our loved ones, we need to rely on the goodwill of the many whom we have aided ourselves. To get cooperation, we have to give it. That's the Law. Since you have scarcely helped others, you can only hope to count on the charitableness of others. But how will you get it, if you aren't able to make friends here? Go back to the Park of Rest now and come back to see me after you've thought all this over for a while."

She dried her eyes at these words—not happy at the disposition of her case, I would think. The Minister looked at me, then, and said, with a new cheer in his voice:

"Your turn, my dear friend."

With that invitation, I prepared myself—somewhat hesitantly, I confess—to present my request.

Chapter Fourteen

CLARENCE EXPLAINS

My heart beat was out of control. Despite the Minister's kindness, I felt like a nervous schoolboy getting ready to take an oral exam from a tough teacher. Thinking about the woman's tears and the Minister's calm but energetic stance, I couldn't feeling hesitant. I was sorry now that I'd set up this interview. Maybe it would have been better to wait until a decision was made about my case at a higher level. Maybe it was presuming too much to ask for a job as a medical doctor at a hospital where I was, after all, still a patient.

The Minister's simple wisdom and directness had opened to me a different perspective. I wished now I could have beaten a retreat back to my room and forgotten all about my hopes of the day before. But I was here and there was no going back. Clarence sensed all of this and, wanting to push me along, said in a firm tone, "Come, come now. Speak up—I'm listening."

Despite not being sure about my qualifications, here I was, all set to ask for a medical position in the colony, when my conscience registered a warning: Why ask for special work?

Did I really want to fall back into that trap again, as I would by asking for a position in keeping with what was once my professional status and education? These thoughts restored my mental equilibrium somewhat and, a bit confused, I began.

"Minister Clarence, I took the liberty of coming today to ask your help in getting some sort of work. Now that my health is back to normal, thanks to the treatment I've received here, I'm beginning to miss my old occupations. Any work you give me will be fine, as long as it keeps me busy."

Clarence gave me a long and intent look, as if he were trying to get beyond the surface words and take the measure of my actual thoughts.

"I see," he said, having evidently seen more than enough. "What you're asking for is just any old kind of work; but deep in your heart, you really miss your consulting room, your patients, the whole atmosphere of the medical profession with which God blessed you on Earth."

I took these words as encouragement and, hopeful, nodded "yes."

After a long pause the Minister said, "You shouldn't forget, though, that God often honors us with a position of trust that we often betray by underestimating the dignity of the calling. For instance, you went to a medical school on Earth that had every facility available to medicine at the time. You never knew the price of a single book—your parents' generosity took care of that and all your other needs. As soon as you graduated, high-paying clients were waiting for you. You didn't have to go through the poor doctor's struggle to build up a practice. Instead, you rose quickly in your career; you had a sterling reputation. But how did you use all those advantages? Unfortunately, to bring about the premature death of your physical body. While you were still young and strong, you abused yourself in the exercise of the profession the Lord gave you."

It was a firm lecture that disturbed me in an odd way.

"Yes, I'm very aware that what you say is true and fair," I said. "But I'd be grateful if you would consider letting me repay my debts by devoting myself to the patients in the Hospital. I would do it with heart and soul."

"A very generous impulse on your part," Clarence said. He was being truthful; sarcasm wasn't part of his makeup. "But you have to remember that the exercise of a profession on Earth is a calling from God. That calling summons its hearers to come into the divine temples of service. However, the meaning of a professional qualification on Earth—for instance, a medical degree— can open up doors to performing amazing deeds of service, but also to all types of abuse. Here, it's more in the nature of an ID card or a work pass. On Earth that card gives the individual carrier the chance to work for the Lord on the planet—that is, if you know its real value. That's true of every profession.

"Now, you were given a medical ID, which means you were admitted into the temple of Medicine. Your actions afterwards, though, don't add up to a strong recommendation. How could I justify sending you out to treat spiritual patients? Your entire professional career on Earth was limited to treating the physical body. Mind you, I'm not denying your competence as a physical healer, but life is more than just the physical body. What would you say about a botanist who bases conclusions about plant life on examinations of the dry bark of a few trees? That's what a medical practice on Earth often amounts to."

I have to confess that I had never heard this high view of professional responsibility before. It was no less amazing that my medical degree could be thought of as an ID card—an admission ticket, if you will, to the zones of work and collaboration with the Lord.

"There's also another problem," Clarence continued. His voice was now as serious as it had ever been. "Most medical doctors on Earth are only interested in charts[10] and test results. They would rather deal with human beings following a mechanical model to their treatments. Now, I agree that physics is a wonderful science, but it's not the only one in the Universe. As you're already aware, doctors ought not to draw the line at somatic diagnoses and medical definitions. They must go deeper, considering the innermost recesses of the soul, where so much physical sickness actually has its origins. But what happens to most of your colleagues on Earth? They become slaves to the conventions of the medical establishment early on. Not many doctors rise above the prejudices of their class and their own self-interest. And when they do, they're usually laughed at by their colleagues, and society quickly follows suit. By all these criteria," he concluded, "you haven't prepared yourself very well for our activities here."

I hardly knew how to answer, so I said simply, "Yes, I understand. What you're saying is absolutely right, I admit it." I was near tears at this point. "But"—summoning all the humility I could— "I'm willing to do anything, Minister, to take any job that will help this blessed

---

[10] Translator's Note: the author used the word Mathematics twice in this paragraph. We took it to imply, in the broadest sense of the word, the quantifiable aspect of medical diagnostics, and the physical laws of the human organism.

sanctuary of peace."

"My dear friend," said Clarence, addressing me in his usual fashion. "You've listened to a few hard truths about yourself just now. I'd like to add a few words of encouragement. You can't become a doctor in Nosso Lar as of this moment. You're simply not ready for it. But eventually I can almost guarantee that you'll be admitted as a medical apprentice. Your present situation here isn't the best, I have to tell you—but it's promising nonetheless. The Ministry of Assistance has received a number of petitions on your behalf."

"My mother?" I asked. The thought filled me with happiness.

"Yes, your mother," the Minister returned. "Your mother—and other friends who remember you and are grateful for what you did for them. Soon after your arrival here, I asked the Ministry of Education to send over your records and notes. I looked them over carefully. What I found was a rash and thoughtless man at times; but I also saw that, in your fifteen years of medical practice, you treated several thousand poor patients for free at your clinic. Usually you did it without thinking about it, sometimes with indifference; but even when your work was mechanical it was a blessing to someone, and that blessing has come back to you, as blessings always do. Fifteen of those patients haven't forgotten you; they've sent in constant appeals on your behalf. I should say that, though you may have forgotten all that you did for them, even that works in your favor.

"Well, you'll learn new lessons here," Clarence said with a smile. "You'll have some experiences that will give you a sense of what's required by our patients. I can see that you'll work with us very well—and at the same time, you'll be preparing yourself for your own ascent toward the Infinite."

These words elated me. For the first time since arriving at the Colony, I cried out of pure happiness. I suspect no one on Earth could have understood the emotions I had at that moment, or appreciated the need I felt to quieten my heart so that I could enter into the sublimity of Divine silence.

Chapter Fifteen

MY MOTHER'S VISIT

I started following Clarence's advice immediately, trying harder to return to full strength so that I could begin my apprenticeship as soon as possible. The Minister's blunt assessment of my condition would have offended me a good deal in my old earthly life. But here, I could only feel comforted. It was clear to me that while immersed in the flesh the soul is wrapped in a dense veil of illusions. It was only now that I realized the full importance of this fact: that life on Earth can't be lived thoughtlessly, as if nothing else mattered. And that is precisely how I had lived mine. Now, the real importance of an incarnation loomed clearly before me. Remembering all the opportunities I had wasted, I couldn't help but be thankful for what Nosso Lar had done for me, and I saw that Clarence had plenty of reasons to speak to me as he did.

Most days I spent deep in thought—and often those thoughts turned to my home on Earth. I longed to visit it, but stopped short of asking for any more favors. My benefactors in the Ministry of Assistance had been extremely generous to me and seemed to anticipate my every wish. So I could only assume that, if they hadn't offered me the chance to visit on their own, it was because the time hadn't arrived for it.

I said nothing, then. Rather, I resigned myself, and soon sadness crept over me. Lisias did his best to cheer me up, trying to engage me in his always lively conversation and giving me a daily word of encouragement. But I was at that stage of spiritual retreat when you retire within yourself to face your innermost conscience.

Then, one day, Lisias came bounding into the room and said, full of excitement, "Guess who's come to see you!"

The smile on his face and in his bright sparkling eyes gave him away.

"My mother!" I shouted.

It could only be her—I was sure of it.

She came into the room holding her arms out to me.

"Andy, Andy!" she called, "Come here! Let me hold you, darling."

It's hard to describe what happened next. Suddenly, I felt like the little kid who used to play in the rain and wandered around barefoot in the sandy soil of our garden. It was a joyful moment, a sacred one. I held her close and gently in my arms, and after a while even our tears blended into each other. I can't say how long we stayed locked together that way, but at last she broke the spell.

"Now, now, sweetheart, calm down," she said, with a little laugh. "All this emotion is going to put a strain on your heart. You're still weak; you need to save up all that strength."

During her last days on Earth I had carried her in my arms; now she was the one who helped me do what I could hardly do for myself. She dried my tears and led me over to the sofa where I sat down beside her and rested my head on her lap. She stroked my hair gently, and began recalling old and precious memories to me— memories that overwhelmed, yet comforted me beyond words. At that moment I was the happiest man in existence. I felt as does a sailor who, having suffered through terrible storms at sea, finds his ship being anchored in the safest harbor in the land.

The comfort she brought my heart was deep. It covered my entire being. "It's like a dream, Mother," I said. "Like a dream of bliss." And like the little boy I had become, looking for solace in all that is familiar and well-loved, I gazed up at her—at her clothes, which reminded me of the dark dress, blue shawl, and woolen stockings she used to wear at home. At her small head, crowned with snow-white hair. At the wrinkles on her face. At her unvarying expression, sweet and calm.

I could find no words for my joy and so, trembling, I stroked her hands.

At the moment she was much the stronger of the two of us. She said quietly, "The Lord never forgets us, Andy. We'll never be able to thank Him enough for all His kindness. Our separation has been long, hasn't it? But don't think I ever forgot you. Not for a moment. It's just that sometimes Providence splits us up for a while so that we can learn the meaning of sublimated Love."

Her affection, I felt, was the same as ever; and as I had often done on Earth, I began to rehearse all my old troubles to her. Such conduct showed me, later, just how hard it is to get rid of our earthly baggage, and how heavy our imperfections, even after the passing of centuries, still weigh on us. Clarence had often urged me to stop all this complaining—so had Lisias. Yet now, as I lay resting in my mother's arms, my old wounds seemed to open and bleed again. My tears of joy gave way to tears of self-pity. I didn't realize, at that moment, that I was supposed to regard her visit not as the mere gratification of my whims, but as one more blessing from the Divine Mercy.

So I fell back into my old habit of making her the victim of my endless problems. It was as foolish an act here as it was on Earth. There, mothers are often no more than slaves in their children's eyes. Not many realize the value of their mother's devotion before they're deprived of it. I was no exception.

My mother listened in silence, an expression of profound sadness on her face. She held me close to her heart, her eyes full of tears.

"Oh, please don't complain, Andy," she said. "Didn't Minister Clarence advise you that you shouldn't? Instead of doing that, let's be thankful to God for the blessing of this meeting after all this time. Let's never forget that we're in a different school now, learning to become true children of God.

"As a mother on Earth, I didn't always guide you in the way I should have. So I'm working to control my old feelings, too; I'm trying to readjust my heart. But when you cry like this and complain, you bring back all those old feelings; and they pull me back on to a road I've already traveled. Oh, I'd like to think that all your complaints are justified—I really would—and that you're the best being in the Universe. But, darling, that wouldn't fit in with the new lessons we're learning here. In the world, I might have been able to excuse your behavior; but here, we must consider the Lord before everything else. You aren't the only discarnate man who's redeeming his past errors, and I'm not the only mother who's been separated from her children. So you have to start looking at your suffering in a new light. What makes suffering valuable aren't the tears it causes us or the wounds it inflicts on us, but the gateway of light it opens up to us. Tears and wounds are only a blessing if they help us purify our souls."

She paused for a while, letting these words sink in. My conscience gave me a good, firm shaking.

"We don't have all that long together," my mother continued, "so let's enjoy the sunshine of love we have. If we keep thinking about our unhappiness, we'll be wasting our time among shadows. It's much better to serve, Andy, and serve with all the cheer we can, and rejoice—always—in God. Please, please change your outlook. The love you have shown me and your trust in my love for you bring me so much happiness—I can't tell you how much. But I can't go back to experiences that have passed. We must love each other now with Divine Love."

These last words inspired and awakened me. My mother's love seemed to radiate with refreshing energies that lifted me up. She saw the change in me and gazed down happily, her face lit up by a bright smile.

I rose and respectfully kissed her on the forehead. It struck me, as I did so, that I'd never seen her look so beautiful and loving.

Chapter Sixteen

A CONFIDENTIAL CONVERSATION

My mother's words comforted and encouraged me considerably. She advised me to work if I needed relief from my sufferings and sorrows—which she viewed, in any case, as valuable lessons. In a strange way, her advice gave me new strength and my spirit suddenly filled with a profound feeling of contentment. I was a different man—livelier, happier, more cheerful.

"The plane you live on must be wonderful, Mother!" I said excitedly. "You must have such sublime thoughts, such bliss!"

She looked at me and smiled her old, knowing smile.

"A higher sphere, Andy," she said, "always requires more work and greater devotion from us— not less. You shouldn't think of me as spending all my time in spiritual ecstasies, having nothing worthwhile to do. Now, I wouldn't want to give you the impression that I'm unhappy with my situation or that it's caused me the least shadow of sadness. I just want you to realize that I have new responsibilities now."

"New responsibilities?" I said

"Yes," she replied simply. "Since I returned from Earth, I've been working constantly for our family's spiritual renewal. When many people leave their physical bodies, they stay tied to their earthly homes; they can't break away from their loved ones. But when I arrived here I learned that the person who truly wants to help her loved ones works nearly all the time in the service of others. That's why I've been trying so hard, ever since my arrival, to earn the right to help out the people both of us love."

"And Father," I asked, "where is he? Why didn't he come with you?"

A troubled expression passed over her face at this question.

"Your poor father," she replied, giving a little sigh. "He's been stuck in a dense section of the Lower Zone for the last twelve years." She broke the news to me directly but as gently as she could manage. "You know how on Earth he always gave us the impression that he was faithful to family values. We believed him a person of great moral integrity, both as a businessman and an individual. We also thought that he had a strong religious faith. Well, none of it was true. The fact is, he was weak. You should know, Andy, that he kept up several clandestine relationships that none of us even guessed at then.

"When Laertes passed over, his stay in the Lower Zone became extremely difficult for him. The spirits of those women were waiting for him, anxious to get him involved in their own lurid illusions. At first he tried to resist them and find me. But he didn't understand that the soul, once it leaves the body, lives out its essential nature. It's naked, so to speak. He couldn't even sense my spiritual presence, and failed to realize that some of our friends were giving him constant help. He spent so many years pretending, you see, that his vibration range dropped very low, and his field of perceptions shrank. Now he's alone with them—the spirits that his heart and mind have become attuned to.

"For a while our family values and a sense of self-respect gave him some strength, and he tried to fight temptation. But finally he gave in. He was attracted back into the indulgences of illusion again. He lacks now, as he lacked then, the ability to persevere, to sustain a worthy mental attitude."

"But isn't there any way of pulling him out of this depravity?" I asked. Her recital of my father's condition had made a painful impression on me.

"Not right now, Andy," she went on. "I visit him all the time, but he isn't even aware that I'm there—his energy pattern is still too low. I try my best to attract him to the right path through inspiration, but the only results so far have been a few occasional tears of repentance—not a single serious resolution."

"And the women around him are no help either, naturally."

"They keep him a prisoner and intercept all my suggestions. Believe me, I've been working intensely on his case for many years, and friends in five different spiritual colonies, including Nosso Lar, have been helping me. Once Minister Clarence almost succeeded in attracting him to the Ministry of Renewal, but it didn't work out. If you don't have the wick or the wax, you can't light the candle. To raise Laertes's perception and free him from his current condition, we have to count on his own willingness. Meanwhile the poor thing is in a state of mental apathy. Part of him lives in anger, part of him just doesn't care."

"And what about Claire and Priscilla?" I asked. These were my sisters.

"Still bound to Earth," came her answer, "living in the Lower Zone. I'm forced to look after everyone's needs. My only direct help has come from your sister Louisa, who passed over while you were still a baby. She's cooperated so lovingly with me! She waited here for years for my arrival, and when it happened, she became my right hand in helping our family on Earth. She was so brave, fighting by my side on behalf of your father, your sisters, and you. But the spiritual turmoil in the family has recently been so serious that last week she went back to Earth—a real gesture of self-denial—to reincarnate among them. Dear, dear Andy," she looked at me with a plea in her eyes, "I hope you'll soon be well so we can work together and do the Lord's work better."

The information about my father had staggered me. What sort of trouble had he been facing? He'd always seemed to take religious duties so seriously, going to communion every Sunday.

Lost in admiration for my mother's devotion, I said, "And you're still doing everything you can to help Father, in spite of his relationship with those low-life women of his?"

"Oh, Andy," she said with a hint of distress in her voice, "please don't call them that—they're God's children, too. It's better to think of them as our sisters who are sick, ignorant, and messed up. I'm not interceding for Laertes just for his sake, but for theirs too, and I think I've found the way to attract all of them to my heart."

Such enormous self-denial on her part filled me with surprise and awe. Then I remembered my own little family, and the old yearning for my wife and children rose up in me again. In Clarence's and Lisias's presence I had managed to keep my feelings in check, never asking questions about them. Now the kind expression on my mother's face encouraged me to speak up. Her visit would probably not last much longer; I had to take advantage of the opportunity while I could.

"Mother, you've been helping Father with such devotion," I said. "Couldn't you give me some news about Celia and the children? I can't wait for the moment when I can go back home and help them. They must miss me as much as I miss them. Poor Celia must be suffering so much from this separation!"

"I see the grandchildren from time to time," she said, giving me a sad little smile. "They're doing just fine." Then, after thinking about it for a few moments she added, "Don't worry too much about your family getting help, Andy. They are fine. Just concentrate on preparing yourself to carry out your mission. There are some questions we simply have to entrust to the Lord; we have to raise our thoughts up to God in faith. It's only then that we can start working to resolve these issues."

Despite this advice, I was anxious to get any information I could and tried to keep my mother on the subject, but she gently changed it again. We then talked for a long time, and her words and the tone of her voice both comforted and soothed me.

I was curious to know where and how she lived, so when she took her leave I asked if I could go with her.

"You mustn't come, Andy dearest" she said, taking my hand in hers and squeezing it affectionately. "I'm due at the Transformation Chambers in the Ministry of Communication very shortly. They'll provide the energy support for my return journey. Besides, I have to go thank Minister Celius for this opportunity to visit you."[11]

She kissed me then, and went out the door. Though gone, she had left in my heart a lasting happiness.

----

[11] *Translator's Note: The energy support referred to here concerns the need to readjust the energies that constitute the spiritual body (or perispirit, as Allan Kardec calls it) to the standards of the realm in which the individual happens to be. The visit of Andy's mother to Nosso Lar, a colony in a lower energy region than her own, required that her spiritual body undergo a densification process. This same issue of difference in vibratory ranges explains the difficulties observed in the communication of spirits with humankind on Earth. Our perceptions on Earth are limited to a narrow range of vibrations, as the physics of sound and color demonstrate. The need mentioned by Andy's mother exists at all levels of the spirit realm whenever there is a significant difference between the vibratory characteristics of two planes or individuals. The difficulty it presents somewhat resembles the difficulties the human body experiences in adapting to high altitudes or deep waters.*

*L*ISIAS'S HOME

A few days after my mother's visit, Minister Clarence summoned me to his office. I was a little surprised at this, but went along gladly with Lisias, who had come to fetch me. The Minister greeted us with the same kindness as always, and I waited for his words with a sense of anticipation.

"My dear Andy," he said cheerfully, "I have some news you'll be glad to hear. From this moment on you may visit, for the purpose of observation and study, all the departments of Nosso Lar except the Ministries of Elevation and Divine Union. Henry de Luna tells me you had your final treatment last week, so it's only right that you spend some time now observing and learning."

Full of excitement, I turned to Lisias. "Did you hear that?" I said, beaming. "Well—of course you did. But—isn't it grand!" He smiled widely, then shot me a glance that gave away his sense of delight at the news.

I was simply overjoyed. It was the beginning of a new life. At long last, I'd be able to join their schools, do meaningful work.

Judging the extent of my happiness, Clarence added, "Now, since your stay in the hospital is no longer necessary, let us give some thought to the question of where you're going to live. In the next day or so, I'll consult some of our institutions and..."

"If it's at all possible, Minister—" Lisias broke in. The tone of Lisias's voice was eager and lively. "I'd like it very much," he continued, with an inquiring look at Clarence, "if Andy could share our home during his period of learning. I assure you, Mother would welcome him like a second son."

At this expression of generosity, I gave my friend a look of thanks. Clarence, in turn, nodded his approval, and not only granted permission but showed his appreciation of the gesture.

"Very well, Lisias," the Minister said. "Jesus rejoices with us whenever we open our hearts to a new friend."

I couldn't find words to express my gratitude at this answer and so hugged my friend close. Great joy sometimes takes away our voices as well as our breath!

"Keep this document with you," Clarence went on. He handed me a small folder. "It will serve as your permit to enter the Ministries of Renewal, Assistance, Communication, and Education for a period of one year. After that, we'll see what else can be done. Don't waste your time, my dear fellow—learn everything you can. Remember that the intervals between our earthly lives must be used wisely."

I left the Minister's office in a state of elation, walking arm in arm with Lisias as if we were two close old friends. We strolled along for several minutes, talking, and then Lisias stopped suddenly at an elegant cottage, which was surrounded by a colorful garden. "Here we are," he announced. "This is our home in Nosso Lar, Andy."

We arrived at the cottage door, and taking me inside Lisias called out a hearty, "Mother! Mother!"

In a few seconds, a pleasant-looking woman appeared from one of the back rooms.

"Mother," Lisias said, with a boyish excitement. "Here's the friend I've been promising you. This is André—Andy."

The woman's face brightened immediately. "Andy! What haven't I heard about you?" she said with genuine affection. "Please," she said softly, "treat this house as your home."

"I understand that your mother doesn't live here," she added, "but you'll find in me a sister who is, let's say"—she nodded toward Lisias—"involved presently in maternal duties."

I didn't know how to thank her for such a reception but I was on the verge of trying when, seeing my intention, she said, "Don't think of saying one word of thanks, my dear Andy. If you do you'll have me remembering all those old rules of deportment we used to learn on Earth, and I'll be flustered beyond belief."

We all laughed. I thought, however, that at least some words were in order. "Very well, I won't mention it," I promised. "But I will say, may the Lord store up my thanks and pour them onto this house in the form of growing peace and joy."

The three of us walked into the cottage's living room then, and I saw my new home for the first time. It was, I noted, simply furnished but comfortable. The furniture, and all the rest of its trappings, resembled those on Earth. From the walls hung paintings of obvious spiritual significance; in one corner stood an unusually large piano, on which sat a harp of very delicate design.

Lisias noticed me looking at the harp and, ready as usual to satisfy my curiosity, said, "As you know, you weren't exactly met by the harpist-angel contingent when you arrived here from Earth. So if you want to know how a heavenly harp sounds, I'm afraid you're going to have to learn to play it yourself!"

"Oh, Lisias, stop your joking around!" his mother said, with mock irritation. "Don't you remember last year when the Ministry of Divine Union invited some of the residents of the Elevation Ministry to hear a group of master harpists who were playing in the Colony?"

"Yes, quite well, Mother," he returned. "Well, let me put it another way: harpists do exist—they really do, Andy— but if you want to hear them you have to develop your sensibility, and the only way you can do that is by seeking the knowledge of divine things."

So our talk went on—full of memories. I told them a little about my history on Earth during my previous incarnation, and in turn I discovered that Lisias's family came from an old town in the state of Rio de Janeiro; that his mother's name was Laura; that his two sisters, Yolanda and Judith, lived here at the cottage with them. This was my first experience of domesticity in the colony, and it delighted me. The atmosphere was homey and tranquil, and it encouraged a sweet and heart-warming intimacy. The family's welcome, all told, stirred deep emotions in me.

As I learned more about the family's life in the colony, I was filled with questions about the latter. Laura, seeing my interest, showed me some wonderful books.

"As far as literature goes," she said, "we have a distinct advantage here in Nosso Lar. You know, there are some writers whose books are only meant to debase minds; all their art does is to poison the psyches of their readers. Here those kinds of writers go straight to the Lower Zone, and as long as they insist on that mind set they can't stay here, not even in the Ministry of Renewal."

She showed me books containing beautiful art work. I couldn't help but smile, and indeed marvel, as I turned the pages. Afterwards, Lisias showed me around the house. Everything was simple, yet obviously designed for comfort.

It was an amazing and elegant little place, and I'd hardly gotten over my wonder when Laura called us to prayer. We were joined now by Yolanda and Judith, and together the five of us sat in silence around a large table in the living room. Soon Laura switched on a large imaging device —a smaller version of the one I had seen by now many times at the hospital. Soft music filled the room; the broadcast was the Government Building's collective prayer service, and its familiar images appeared before us. In the background the blue heart appeared, and at the sight of it I was filled with a deep and mysterious happiness; indeed, at that moment, my whole soul was alive with joy and gratitude.

Chapter Eighteen

$\mathcal{L}$OVE, THE NOURISHMENT OF SOULS

$\mathcal{P}$rayer was soon over, and not long afterwards Laura called us for a light repast. On the table sat a tureen of appetizing soup and a selection of delicious-smelling fruits piled up on a large platter. The latter tasted more like a blend of concentrated liquids than the pulpy variety of fruit I was used to on Earth, but they were nonetheless exquisitely delicious.

"Our meals are a lot better here than on Earth, don't you think?" Laura said. "Of course, some districts do without them altogether, but in certain areas of the Ministry of Assistance we can't do that. The kind of work we do—assisting individuals in dense circles of the Lower Zone—takes up too much energy. So we depend on various forms of concentrates. We must make sure that our bodies are well sustained."

At this point, Yolanda, one of the sisters, spoke up. "That doesn't mean, though, that those of us who work at Assistance and Renewal are the only ones who depend on some form of nutrition for our bodies; the other Ministries—even Divine Union—use it too. The only difference among Ministries is the form of the nourishment. In Communication and Education it most commonly takes the form of fruits; in Elevation, it's mostly juices and concentrated fluids. As for the Ministry of Divine Union...well, the process of nutrition there is simply beyond imagination."

This information left me more eager for an explanation than ever. I turned my eyes from Yolanda to her mother. Everyone at the table smiled at my natural curiosity; but Laura soon resolved my confusion:

"You may not be aware yet, Andy," she said, "that love is the strongest sustaining force among all of God's creatures. From time to time, large delegations of instructors visit our city to teach the principles of spiritual nutrition; and what we've learned from them primarily is that love is the fundamental basis for nutritional systems throughout the Universe. If you look at physical diet in the right way you see that it's always a question—even here—of a passing phase of materiality. We need it just as automobiles on Earth need grease, oil, and gas. But love, and love only, is the source of nourishment for the soul, and the further along on the evolutionary path of Creation we are, the better we understand that fact. Divine Love is the mainspring of the Universe, don't you agree?"

I was very much comforted by these explanations, and even more so when Lisias added, "God's infinite love is the center of equilibrium for all Creation. The more evolved a being is, the more subtle is its nutrition process. Worms in the ground feed mostly on earth; larger animals find their nourishment in plants. Human beings gather the fruits of these plants and prepare them to suit their individual tastes. Those of us who are already free of our physical bodies need energy-filled substances in more rarefied forms. The processes become more subtle, more delicate, the farther along we go in our ascent."

"But let's not forget the medium of life too soon," Laura continued. "The fact is that worms, animals, humans on Earth, and we ourselves depend entirely on love. We all move about in it; in fact, life would be impossible without it. Don't you remember Jesus's words in the Gospel: 'Love one another'?[12] When he said that, he wasn't just referring to charity in the strict sense of the word, because all of us have to learn, sooner or later, that giving—doing good—is simply our duty. No, he primarily wanted us to understand His words in the broader sense. That is to say, we're to sustain each other through mutual love and empathy. In the future, human beings will discover that tender words, mutual kindness and trust, understanding and friendly interest—all of which are the fruit of genuine love—are really the most stimulating food that life can take in. Naturally, when we're on Earth, obstructed by our physical natures, we operate

----

[12] *Translator's Note: John 13:34 "A new command I give you: Love one another. As I have loved you, so you must love one another."*

under huge limitations that prevent us from seeing this clearly. But once we're back here, we know. We realize that lasting happiness and contentment are actually a matter of purely spiritual sustenance. Homes, villages, towns, and nations everywhere are built according to principles like this."

While she was talking, I found myself remembering different theories about the nature and meaning of love and sex that are widely held in the physical world. Laura seemed to guess these thoughts.

"No, Andy," she said, "you shouldn't think that it's all simply a matter of sex. Sex is a sacred expression of universal and Divine love. But it's only one of many expressions of that love's potential, which is infinite. Actually, more spiritualized couples find that tenderness, trust, mutual devotion, and understanding count for much more than physical relations. Sex very often becomes a transitory activity for them. In general, we can say that the exchanges of emotional intimacy establish necessary rhythms for the existence of harmony. For such couples the mere presence of the loved one, and sometimes a simple understanding, is enough to nourish their joy."

At this point, Lisias's other sister, Judith, took up the thread of the conversation.

"We learn here in Nosso Lar," she said, "that life on Earth finds its point of equilibrium in love. But most incarnate people never realize the extent of truth in that statement. Twin, friendly, and empathetic souls form pairs and groups of every kind. They come together and help each other, and in this way sustain themselves in their projects of redemption. Take away that help and a weaker person usually fails before completing the journey."

"As you see, Andy," Lisias added, "even here we're reminded of the lesson in the Gospel, 'One cannot live by bread alone.'"[13]

Our talk was interrupted now by the ringing of the doorbell. Lisias got up to answer it, and a few seconds later ushered in two polite young fellows, Polydor and Eustacius. They were, he said, friends from the Ministry of Education. We stood up and introduced ourselves; handshakes followed all around. After a few minutes, Laura said with a smile, "Well, I can imagine that you've all worked

---

[13] Translator's Note: Matthew 4:4 "It is written: 'Man does not live on bread alone, but on every word that comes from the mouth of God.'"

hard today, so don't change your plans on our account. I know very well that you're going to the Music Fields, and I suspect it's time you started out."

At these words Lisias's face wore the uneasy look of a conflicted man.

"Oh, go along, my love—don't keep Lavinia waiting," Laura said. "Our friend Andy will stay with me until he can go with you on your outings."

"Oh please, don't stay on my account!" I exclaimed.

"I can't enjoy the pleasure of going to the Music Fields just yet," Laura told us. "My granddaughter returned from Earth a few days ago, and she's still much too weak to go out."

The small group walked out of the house talking to each other happily. Laura shut the door behind them, and turning to me said, "They're going in search of the nourishment we were talking about just now. The ties of love are stronger and more beautiful here. Love, Andy, is the divine bread of the soul, the true nourishment of the heart."

*T*HE NEWCOMER

"*D*oesn't your granddaughter come down for meals?" I asked Laura.

"For the moment she takes her meals alone," she replied. "The dear child is still run down—a nervous wreck—and no one in that condition is supposed to share in collective meals. The fact is that nervous exhaustion and excessive sorrow send out a dense, noxious energy that immediately mixes with the food."

"She spent two weeks in the Lower Zone in a deep sleep," she said. "We watched over her the whole time. Ordinarily, of course, she would've been taken to a hospital, but it was decided instead to place her directly under my care."

"I'd be delighted to visit her, if I might," I told Laura.

"Oh, would you?" she returned, "I think she'd love the company."

She took me then to a large and comfortable bedroom where we found a pale-faced young woman sitting in an easy-chair. Seeing a stranger enter her room, the young woman gave me a look of surprise just verging on puzzlement.

"Lois," Laura said softly, "here's a friend who just arrived from Earth a little while ago."

Lois's curiosity was roused, but her tired eyes, under which I could see black circles, showed what an effort it was for her to concentrate. She gave me a wan little smile.

"Hello," I said, trying to project a little cheerfulness in my voice. "My name is André. Most people call me Andy. You must be tired ..."

Before Lois could answer, Laura, as if anxious to take as much strain off her granddaughter as she could, addressed me calmly.

"Lois has been restless and worried," she explained. "And to some extent her fear has a solid basis. Her life on Earth ended due to tuberculosis. Her long suffering left deep traces in her spiritual body. Still, we have to be optimistic and brave—don't we, Lois?"

At this, the young lady opened her deep, baggy eyes as if to hold back tears. The effort was unsuccessful. She held her pose for one second, covered her face with her hand, and sobbed.

"Poor sweet little thing!" said Laura. She put her arms around the crying girl and comforted her. "Oh, please try to get hold of yourself, dear," she said soothingly. "All these troubles are the result of a bad religious education, that's all. You know that your mother won't be long in coming. And I know it's hard to accept, but you can't count on your fiancé being faithful. You know you can't. It isn't in him to offer you sincere spiritual devotion from Earth. He's a long way from having that kind of spiritual love. You have to get used to the idea that he's certain to marry somebody else. Besides, it wouldn't be fair to insist on bringing him here before his time."

Laura gave me a resigned look and went on talking in gentle tones to her granddaughter.

"And suppose we could bend the law and he did come," she said. "Wouldn't you end up suffering even more? Wouldn't you have to pay a heavy price for your share in causing him to abandon his life plan? Here you have devoted friends, brothers and sisters, who'll help restore your spiritual health, and if you really love this boy, you'll cooperate with them and try to adopt a more harmonious attitude. That way you'll be able to help him later. Besides, as I've already said, your mother will soon be here. Doesn't that make you just a little happier?"

The girl's tears filled me with pity. I tried changing the subject—anything to lead the conversation away from a memory that was obviously very painful to her.

"Where do you come from?" I asked.

Laura, now silent, took the opposite tactic from the one of a moment before; she seemed anxious that her granddaughter join in the conversation. Lois, after a pause to dry her eyes, said, "From Rio de Janeiro."

"You shouldn't cry like this, Lois." I advised. "You don't know how lucky you've been. You passed over only a few days ago, and already you're with your family. You didn't have to face any storms on the great journey, as many do."

She seemed a little more composed now.

"You can't imagine how much I've suffered," she said. "Eight months struggling with tuberculosis, in spite of all the treatments... and there was the pain of knowing I infected my mother. And all my poor fiancé went through because of me! It's really undescribable."

"Dearest, please don't say things like that," Laura said. "On Earth we always seem to think that no suffering is greater than ours—but it's an illusion, simple blindness. There are millions of creatures facing situations that are much harsher and more cruel than the ones that make up our little experiences."

"But, grandmother, Arnold was so heart-broken, so—desperate," she answered. "It's all so hard to understand."

"Do you really believe your view of him tells the whole truth, Lois?" Laura asked. Her voice had grown more tender than it had been since we entered the room. "I watched your ex-fiancé several times while you were sick," she continued. "Naturally he was deeply upset to see the tuberculosis ruining your body. But let me tell you again, he can't understand feelings in their higher form. He'll soon get over his grieving. Remember, dear, that real love, enlightened love, is still above most human beings. What you must do now is try to be of good cheer—the sooner that happens the sooner you'll be able to help Arnold. But don't expect him to be faithful to your memory; it's out of the question. When you're in a condition to visit the planet, you'll find him married to somebody else."

While Lois gave her a look of pained surprise, I found myself wondering about the situation myself. Clearly, she didn't know how to react to her grandmother's serenity and common sense in this situation.

"It's not possible!" she blurted out.

Laura stroked the girl's hair, giving her as much comfort as she could.

"Now, Lois, please don't be stubborn or try to contradict me, my dear."

She saw, though, that her granddaughter expected some explanation for this charge against Arnold's faithfulness.

"Do you remember Maria," Laura continued, "your girlfriend

from college who brought you flowers every Sunday? Well, when the doctor finally announced, in confidence, that your condition was incurable, Arnold began to involve her in thoughts which were different from the ones he had had in the past. Oh, he grieved a great deal for you—don't think he didn't. But now that you're here, it isn't going to take very long until something more profound happens between them."

"Oh, Grandma!"—her voice was suddenly much stronger— "that's so awful!"

"Why is it awful?" asked Laura. "You have to get used to considering other people's needs in these cases, Lois. Your ex-fiancé is an ordinary man. He isn't able to appreciate the beauty of spiritual love right now. No matter how great your love may be, you can't work miracles in him. Every creature has the right—the exclusive right— to discover his or her own inner self. One of these days, Arnold will know and understand how beautiful your idealism is. But for now he has to live through these necessary experiences, and we have to let him."

"I simply can't get over it!" Lois held her hands to her face and shook her head back and forth. "I always considered Maria my best friend," she said in a tone of exasperation.

"Then won't it be better to trust him to a friend?" Laura asked. "Maria will always be your spiritual friend. Another woman might make it a great deal harder for you to relate with him later on."

Lois started sobbing again. I was very puzzled myself, which Laura sensed, and eager to help both of us, told her granddaughter, "I know why you're crying, baby. And you shouldn't think that your Grandma is trying to hurt you—she's just trying to open your eyes when she tells you this. It is a feeling that comes from centuries of abandoning the soil of the spirit to the weeds of conceit and selfishness."

With these words, Laura motioned for me to come back to the living room. "Let's leave Lois alone for a while, Andy," she told me. "She needs her rest." And so we left her there for the time being, still crying.

Later, as we sat waiting for the others to come back, Laura took me even further into the family's confidence. "When my granddaughter arrived here, she was extremely tired," she said. "She had let her heart get tangled up in the web of self-love. To tell you the truth, she should have been sent to one of our hospitals. But Assistant Cocero thought tender loving care on our part would be the best course in her case. I have to say I was pleased at the decision, especially since my dear Theresa, her mother, will soon be here. A little patience and everything will work out all right. It's just a question of time and a calm atmosphere."

Chapter Twenty

*N*OTIONS ABOUT THE HOME

*L*aura seemed to be a fountain of information, and since I was eager to learn as much as possible, she quickly found herself swept up in a whole series of questions.

"You have so much to do at home," I said. "Do you still work outside it?"

"I certainly do," she replied. "We live in a transition colony — apprenticeship and work are its main purposes. Here, women always find themselves doing a number of different tasks; it's to prepare them for going back to the planet or to rise to the higher spheres."

"What about domestic arrangements in Nosso Lar? Are they like the ones on Earth?"

"Actually, without realizing it, married couples on Earth have, for a very long time, been trying to reach and imitate the domestic ideal we've attained in the spirit realms. But couples there are still weeding the garden of their feelings. There are rare exceptions, but most find themselves surrounded by the bitter herbs of pride; they've become infested with those old parasites, jealousy and selfishness. Here things take on a different perspective. The last time I returned from the planet, for instance, I naturally arrived absorbed in deep illusions. But during a crisis of wounded pride, I was taken to a lecture given by a great instructor from the Ministry of Education. Since then, a new current of ideas has taken root in my mind."

"What kind of things did he say?" I asked with great curiosity.

"The lecturer," she continued, "was a great mathematician. He made us realize that, on the path of spiritual evolution, a home can be compared to a right angle. The vertical line of the angle represents the feminine mentality, which always moves toward life's creative inspirations. The horizontal line is the masculine mentality, which always strives to bring about the common good. A home is the sacred intersection between these two lines; it's where man and woman meet to bring about an essential understanding between their two mentalities. It is the temple where they ought to reach for spiritual communion rather than only physical union."

"That's a very high conception of marriage," I said.

"At the moment there are a great many people on Earth who are well-versed in social sciences, and who advocate a renovation of domestic life. Some of them go so far as to say that the family as an institution is threatened. But we have to remember that humanity is only slowly gaining the victories over itself that will make a more ideal home life possible. Where can you find, on Earth, a real family structure—one where rights and duties are equally shared?

"Most couples on Earth pass their lives together apathetically or otherwise very selfishly. When the husband is calm, the wife stirs up some spat; when the wife keeps quiet, the husband throws his weight around. She doesn't encourage him along the horizontal line, where his earthly fulfillment lies; he doesn't try to follow in her divine flights of tenderness and feeling toward the higher planes of Creation. When they're out in public both of them wear masks; when they're at home, the masks come off, and their lack of real togetherness becomes painfully obvious.

"Often it's a matter of thoughtlessness. Often, when one of them is talking about their day's activities, the other tunes out completely. Whenever this kind of mental sabotage happens, the lines of the divine angle are no longer intersecting. What we see instead are two lines trying to form a point of intersection but diverging from each other so that neither partner is able to take the next step up the stairway that leads to eternal life."

This new perspective on the responsibilities of marriage struck a deep chord in me. I was very much impressed and couldn't help showing my enthusiasm. "So many thoughts! Your explanation is stirring so many thoughts in me. If we only knew all this while we were on Earth!"

"It's largely a matter of experience, Andy" she replied. "Trials and suffering will gradually teach inescapable lessons like this to all human beings. Right now, only a few humans realize that the home is a divine institution, that we should try to live within it with all our hearts and souls. It's often said that all human beings are beautiful when they're genuinely in love. Well, it's true, and especially during the engagement period, when both partners are on their best behavior and show their best sides. Any subject that one brings up in a conversation, even the silliest one, seems to enchant the other. They meet and radiate all their finest energies to the fullest. But as soon as they're married, they stop desiring each other's hearts and fall in the arms of the old demons that hide in the heart. Suddenly tolerance is gone, and they stop cooperating as they once did. Love in all its bright beauty gradually dies out. The couple begins to drift apart; they avoid each other's company and lose the delight they once took in friendly conversation. From that point on, the more polite ones will respect each other; the other ones will simply fight, in private and in public. They won't try to reconcile or come to any kind of friendly understanding; they'll only speak to each other in cold, dry phrases. They might still continue to share a physical life, but their minds will already be divorced and going in opposite directions."

"Everything you say is so very true!" I said, with feeling.

"But what can we do, Andy?" my hostess continued. "In the present evolutionary stage on the planet, marriages between twin souls are rare. Marriages between friendly or even empathetic souls are greatly outweighed by the remarkable percentage of 'probation ties.' Most couples are two prisoners handcuffed to each other."

Laura now came back to my first question about women's work.

"Women[14] cannot remain inactive here," she said. "It's necessary to learn to fulfill the roles of missionary, sister, mother, wife. But we also learn that a woman's contribution to the household can't be limited to a few tears of pity and years of slaving for other people. Of course, a desperate, ill-thought feminist movement is really an

----

[14] *Translator's Note: The statements about feminism and a woman's position in society espoused by Laura reflect her personal views. The reader should keep it in mind that the events described in the book took place in the late 1930s. André Luiz is simply reporting the views expressed by Laura. Her views clearly reveal her personal concepts and indirectly the societal views that marked the early part of the twentieth century. From reference dates indicated elsewhere, we may safely infer that her last life on Earth must have occurred between 1860-1910.*

offense to the true qualities of the feminine spirit. Women aren't meant to set themselves up as rivals to men in offices or in the different professions and businesses, fields which fall naturally along the line of masculine activity in our right angle example. Still, we're taught in the Colony that there are many careers outside the home that are very compatible both with feminine sensibility and dignity—nursing, teaching, communications, social work, and any kind of occupation which requires patience. In the home itself, men learn to bring the fruit of their world experience, while women contribute by lightening the burden of the man's hard, work creating a tranquil, inspiring atmosphere. Within the family circle, inspiration; outside of it, activity. You can't have one without the other. How could a river keeping flowing without its source? And where would the water of the source flow to without the river bed?"

I couldn't help smiling at this last colorful metaphor. Laura next turned the conversation toward herself, trying to give me a sense of true feminine qualities. "Whenever the Ministry of Assistance entrusts children to my care, my working hours count double. That gives you an idea of how important motherhood should be seen on Earth. But whenever I'm not occupied with children at home, I have my everyday job in the Nursing Department to attend to. Except for my granddaughter, who's still recovering, no member of our family is idle; they're all engaged in one worthwhile activity or another. An eight hour workday is an easy program for anybody. I'd feel ashamed if I didn't do my part."

She was silent for a few moments, and I let my thoughts run now in a different direction.

Chapter
Twenty-One

AN INTERESTING CONVERSATION

"You bring up lots of questions, Laura," I said. "I hope you're not offended by all this curiosity ..."

"Oh, not at all," she replied warmly. "Go on asking, please. I might not be in a condition to teach you, but I can always inform you!"

Both of us laughed at this remark and, taking my cue from her, I asked, "What about private property here in the colony? For instance, does this house belong to you?"

"Well," she replied, "just as on Earth, private property is relative here. We acquire the right to use property on the basis of working hours. The "hour-bonus" is our currency, which we earn through our own efforts and devotion. We can use them as a means of exchange for whatever we need. Generally speaking, the buildings represent a common inheritance, administered by the colony's government. But spiritual families can obtain a house — never more than one per family — upon presenting thirty-thousand hour-bonuses, which they can earn over a specific period of work.

"My husband arrived here long before I did, and he obtained this residence through a great deal of determined effort. We were physically separated for eighteen years, although we stayed united in spirit. Richard didn't waste time here. As soon as he came to Nosso Lar, after a period of considerable upset, he realized the necessity for work, and set about preparing our future. When I arrived, we settled together in this house, which he'd worked for with love, and we were truly happy. My husband then set out to teach me everything he'd learned.

"When I was widowed, I was still a young woman," Laura con-

tinued. "The responsibility of raising several small children had fall-
en on my shoulders, and I had to struggle hard to meet it. I worked
constantly, and gave my children the best education I could give
them, though at an early age they got used to hard work themselves.
But on the whole it was a good experience. I later came to see that
the tough life I led actually protected me from a number of insidious
temptations, and the consequent suffering and anguish later in the
spirit life. Indeed, it saved me from spending any time in the Lower
Zone. I can tell you, Andy, that having a healthy occupation and getting physically tired in the pursuit of it are valuable ways of shelter-
ing yourself and creating an opportunity for your soul to grow spiritually."

I mulled over this new thought for a moment.

"Meeting Richard again and resuming our life together in a new
home was wonderful. For many years we led a life of undisturbed
joy here, growing closer and closer to each other. And we worked —
not only for our own improvement, but for the progress of others
also. After a time, Lisias, Yolanda and Judith also joined us, and our
happiness was even greater."

Finishing her story, she seemed wrapped in thought for a
moment, and when she continued, it was on another level altogether.

"Earth waits for us, however," she said in a serious tone. "The present might be a joy, but the past requires correction from us so that
the future will be in harmony with the Eternal Law. Hour-bonuses
won't pay our debts on Earth; we have to do that ourselves—with
the sweat of our brow. But the time we spend here helps us a lot: due
to our goodwill, our perceptions concerning the mistakes of the past
grow constantly clearer. We understand, then, that the Eternal Law,
which is unfailing in its rhythms, makes our return to the planet
absolutely necessary."

I was deeply impressed by these explanations. Since I had arrived
in the colony, it was the first time that anyone had ever talked to me
with such forcefulness about the subject of past lives.

"Laura," I said, wanting to know more, "pardon my interrupting,
but I'm really curious about why, up to this point, I haven't had an
inkling about my previous lives. I'm free from physical bonds, aren't
I? Haven't I crossed the river of death? Did you remember your past

lives immediately afterwards, or did it take some time with you, too?"

"I certainly had to wait," she answered. She smiled, I thought, at the memory of that time. "First you have to get rid of all your physical impressions. The layers of inferior traits are extremely thick, you know, and you need to be well-centered if you're going to recollect your lives in a constructive way. As a rule, we've all made obvious errors in the cycles of eternal life—and those errors carry over. The memory of having committed a crime makes the criminal the unhappiest person in the Universe; the memory of having been a victim makes the victim feel as if the sin committed against him or her is the greatest wrong ever done. Therefore, the only individuals who are allowed spontaneous recall are those who are surest of themselves, spiritually speaking. A limit is put on the recall of others for their own well-being; if they try to go beyond it, they usually become more emotionally unbalanced and might even go insane."

"But you did remember your past in the natural course of things?"

"I'll tell you," she went on patiently. "After I arrived here, as my inner vision gradually became clearer, vague memories of those lives began stirring in the depths of my mind. Believe me, Andy, they caused me great mental pain. My husband was suffering from the same condition, so together we decided to consult Assistant Lombardi. He examined our memory patterns carefully and then sent us to the specialists over in the Ministry of Education. They took us to the Archives Department, where all our private files are located. These specialists then advised us to spend as much spare time as we could over there for the next two years, reading our own archives. Those archives spanned three centuries. Actually there were more, but the director of the Recollection Service wouldn't let us go back beyond that time because the recollection of those very early eras would be too much for us."

"Were the archives enough to help you remember your past?"

"No, the reading only gave us the bare facts. So after a long period of meditation that was intended to arouse our own inner realization, we were—to our great surprise—put through a series of therapies. These were aimed at reconnecting us with the emotional field of our recollections. Specialists in the subject gave our minds magnetic treatments. These treatments were designed to arouse certain latent energies within us, and only when this happened could we remember in detail approximately three hundred years of life on Earth. We realized then the extent of our debts to our generous planet."

"And where is Richard at the moment?" I said, truly intrigued by the thought of such an extraordinary person. "I'd love to meet him!"

Laura shook her head sadly.

"In light of what we came to know about the past, we planned a new meeting on Earth where we have a great deal of work left to do. Richard left Nosso Lar three years ago. I'll follow him very shortly. I'm just waiting for Theresa to come back so that I can leave her in charge."

She stared into the distance for a moment, as if her thoughts were far away with her husband and daughter on Earth.

"Lois's mother won't be long in coming," she said. "Her passage through the Lower Zone will last only a few hours. She'll be able to do without treatment at the Ministry of Renewal because of the intense suffering she's gone through on Earth, so I can pass my work in the Ministry of Assistance on to her and depart in peace. The Lord won't forget us."

Chapter
Twenty-Two

*T*HE HOUR BONUS[15]

*A*s I said, at the mention of her husband, Laura's expression had suddenly become sad. I decided it was time to change the subject to something less personal.

"What about the 'hour-bonus'?" I asked, "Is it some kind of currency or what?"

Laura's expression changed quickly, and with yet another explanatory duty before her, she came back to the present.

"No, not exactly money, "she answered, looking for the best words to describe it. "It's more like—uh—an individual service coupon. With purchasing power."

"Purchasing power?" I asked.

"Why not?" she continued. "In Nosso Lar, producing nutritional products and other supplies is a community activity. The Government Building runs distribution departments that supply the various Ministries. In the Ministries, there's a central storehouse, which holds all supplies. Everyone cooperates in the process as a

----

15 *Translator's Note: The hour-bonus is simply an internal control procedure used in Nosso Lar. Given Nosso Lar's proximity to Earth, the strong identification of its inhabitants with the physical life, and its purely transitional aspect as a colony—most individuals are preparing for reincarnation—it employs practices that resemble Earth's. Institutions in other spheres likely employ different systems.*

From a more fundamental perspective, love is the only currency that represents value in the Universe. The bonus-hours acquired during service in Nosso Lar are only an indirect and indicative measure of time committed to service, rather than love. Unlike worldly concepts of currency, in the realms of Spirit one's love worthiness is expressed in the purity of one's inner light, rather than in terms of stored units of measure.

matter of public good, since we all depend on it for our provisions. But the workers are given certain privileges—it all depends on their individual merit. Naturally, all the colony's citizens get a basic provision of food and supplies, but the ones who earn hour-bonuses are entitled to certain privileges.

"For instance, individuals who don't work can still find shelter here, but only those who cooperate for the well-being of the colony can have their own private homes. Non-workers get essential clothing; the most devoted ones can satisfy their own tastes in clothes. Non-workers can find a place in our rest-homes or hospital parks; but only hard-working individuals who strive to gain hour-bonuses can enjoy the company of their loved ones at their own leisure or attend different schools.

"All of us have to learn to value the significance of each step in our spiritual ascent," said Laura. "Each individual on the colony's working staff gives at least eight hours of useful service a day. But there's a great deal to do in the different sectors, so the Government House allows those who are really willing to cooperate to put in four extra hours per day. This way, it's possible to earn as many as seventy-two hour-bonuses a week, excluding those earned in difficult missions. These missions, incidentally, offer double pay—sometimes triple."

"And the hour-bonus is the only form of payment?"

"It's the only one we have here. And it's applied to all workers in Nosso Lar, no matter what kind of job."

At this, I thought of the way businesses and bureaucracies are organized on Earth, and asked, "But how can you reconcile the payment with the nature of the work? If a Minister, for instance, receives eight hour-bonuses in an ordinary day, does an aide receive the same? Doesn't the Minister's work have a higher intrinsic value than the aide's?"

Laura smiled at the question, knowing the kind of arguments this would have caused back on Earth.

"That all depends," she began. "If the work calls for sacrifice and self-denial, the payment is decided on a corresponding basis, whether the worker's position is a responsible or humble one. But to give you a more intelligent answer we must first get rid of certain earthly prejudices about work. As you can imagine, the nature of work is an enormously important problem everywhere. But Earth is the only place where its solution gets us tangled up in so many problems. Most incarnates, Andy, are still trying out their first steps in the spirit of service. They're learning the simplest, most elementary lessons on how to perform their missions in life. It's essential, for that reason, that payments be fixed with painstaking care. It's sad, though, that so few there treat material earnings as the transitory things they are. So many people become obsessed by salaries and profits. Often, when they die, they leave huge fortunes behind, and their heirs come along and spend it all without a second thought. Other people build up large bank accounts, then do nothing but worry about them. And of course that much money usually starts fights in their families after they're gone.

"On the other hand, we have to keep in mind that 70 percent of executives on Earth have no idea of the ethical responsibilities that come with their positions—and we can say the same thing about an approximately equal percentage of the workers in their organizations. Most of them spend their lives complaining about how little satisfaction they get from their careers, but it would never occur to them to doubt that they have a right to the salaries that come with their positions, no matter how badly they fill them.

"Governments and hospitals hire workers and doctors who disregard their sacred duty, who turn their energies into other channels or engage in 'killing time'. What happens to the spirit of service under those circumstances?

"In every sector of public life, at every level, you find 'experts' who never fully realize the extent of their responsibilities. They're like poisonous flies landing on sacred bread; they'll find some law and use it to claim all kinds of facilities, bonuses, and pensions for themselves. They'll pay a bitter price for that kind of activity, you can be sure. Earth's society seems to be a long way off from being able to evaluate the real quality of someone's work; but in the higher spiritual plane, service is never assessed without considering the quality of personal effort that went into it."

Laura's words had set off a new train of thought in me, and reading the interest in my face, she pursued the subject a few steps further.

"Real profit, the only profit that matters, is spiritual in nature. In our organization the actual value of the hour-bonus depends on the nature of the work you do. Thus, at the Ministry of Renewal, there are Renewal hour-bonuses; at the Ministry of Education, there are Education hour-bonuses, and so on. Spiritual merit is always valued accordingly, so our individual work records are very specific about the essence of our work.

"In reality, the hour-bonus method is just a record-keeping system. The real 'profit,' if you want to call it that, is experience and knowledge, an increase in Divine blessings, and more opportunities. From this viewpoint, effort and self-denial are by far the most important factors. As a rule, most of us in the colony are preparing ourselves for our return to Earth. So if someone devotes five thousand hours to good works, this person will have built up a great quantity of effort on his or her own behalf. Someone who's worked six thousand hours in the Ministry of Education should be all the wiser for that effort on Earth. Naturally, we can exchange hour-bonuses for whatever we want. But our individual file, the one that records the time we spend in useful service, is a much more valuable asset. It entitles us to all sorts of privileges."

This clarification paved the way to still another question.

"And can we spend hour-bonuses on behalf of friends?" I asked.

"Certainly," Laura answered, "we can share the fruit of our labors with anyone we want. It's an inalienable right of every devoted worker. Thousands and thousands of individuals here in Nosso Lar have benefitted from that sharing."

"In the form of intercessions—is that right?" (I was thinking about the intercessions that had been made for me.)

"Yes, in the form of intercessions. The longer our useful service has been, the more intercessions we're allowed. Andy, we come to see in Nosso Lar that everything has its value, and that to receive we have to give. So mutual assistance is very important here; it's one of the most significant threads that holds the fabric of our lives together. We also come to understand that only those of us who've achieved a certain spiritual level are in a position to ask favors and give help."

"And is there such a thing as inheritance?" I said.

"Oh, it's a pretty simple matter here," she told me with a laugh. "For instance, in my own case, the time to return to the physical plane is very near. At present I have three thousand Assistance hour-bonuses in my account. I can't give them to my daughter, who's about to arrive, because they revert back to the community once I'm gone. The only thing my family will actually inherit is the use of this home. But my service record certainly entitles me to intercede on my daughter's behalf. It can help her get work in the colony as well as friendly care. And it will guarantee me precious assistance from the colony's organizations during my stay on Earth. In addition, I'll return to Earth with a much higher standard of values—my real profit— thanks to years of cooperation in the Ministry of Assistance. That experience should contribute to what I hope will be success in my new life."

Compared to what happened on Earth, this process of earning, profiting, cooperating and serving was both simple and admirable, and I was about to say as much when I heard the sound of hushed voices outside the house. Before I could open my mouth, Laura declared, "Our dear ones are back already."

And she went to the door to welcome them.

Chapter Twenty-Three

*T*HE ART OF LISTENING

*L*aura's explanations were so stimulating to my heart that I couldn't help feeling sorry about the interruption in our conversation. But Lisias had come back in good spirits."

"Hello! Haven't you gone to bed yet?" he asked, slapping me on the back and flashing a grin.

The two young men I'd met earlier took their leave, and Lisias invited me to come outside.

"You haven't seen the moonlight from these surroundings," he said.

I followed him into the garden, leaving Laura to talk to her daughters. It really was a magnificent sight. I had grown used to the hospital grounds, set in a grove of large trees, and this was my first chance to marvel at the wonderful spectacle of a moonlit night from the spacious quarters of the Ministry of Assistance. The garden itself added greatly to the effect: exquisitely colored gloxinias were banked along the sides of the fence, providing a vivid background for beds of fragrant, snow-white lilies, all tinged by a slight blue at the base of their blossoms.

I drew in a deep breath and felt a wave of new energy fill my whole being. In the distance, the towers of the Government Building rose up gracefully, each bathed by beams of light. Admiration hushed me into silence for a moment; in fact, some time passed before I managed to speak at all:

"What a night! I've never had such a peaceful feeling!" I declared to Lisias.

"That's because all the well-centered citizens of the colony have pledged to avoid sending out negative thought-waves," he told me. "The efforts of the majority merge into one and what results is an almost continual prayer. That's where the feeling of peace comes from."

For a time we gazed in wonder at the soul-stirring scenery, trying to take in all we could of the night's many-colored lights and its soothing calm. We went back into the living room then, and Lisias started playing with the dials of a small imaging device. My curiosity was instantly roused.

"What are we going to hear? Messages from Earth?"

"No, we aren't going to hear anything from Earth — most definitely not," he told me, then explained, "Our broadcasts use high frequency waves that are much subtler than those used on Earth."

"But isn't there any way of picking up Earth broadcasts, too?" I asked.

"Of course there is," Lisias replied. "They do it all the time in the Ministries. But at home we only concern ourselves with our condition here and what we're doing now. Work programs in different departments, news from more evolved spheres, and sacred teachings are a lot more important to us than problems on Earth."

It was a just remark. But I was still wrapped up in my own family ties and couldn't help pushing the matter further.

"You really think so? What about the relatives we left behind? Our parents? Our children?"

"I was expecting that question," Lisias answered. "You see, Andy, on the material plane, we often misinterpret situations. There, most of us suffer from a kind of emotional over-response. We become slaves to our "clan" and tend to limit our family to blood relatives. We go through life paying very little attention to the true principles of friendship. We preach them to everyone, but when it comes to putting them into practice, nothing counts but our own flesh and blood. Life takes on a different aspect here, though. We have to conquer our old weaknesses and correct our old injustices.

"We're told that in the colony's early days every home had equipment that picked up broadcasts from Earth. Can you guess what happened? Everybody insisted on hearing news about their relatives who were still there and, from the Ministry of Renewal all the way to Elevation, just about everybody in Nosso Lar lived with their

nerves on edge. There constantly were disturbing rumors that inter-
fered with the good order of the place. Sometimes whole families
were thrown into utter chaos because they heard bad news about
their loved ones on Earth. If a serious problem happened there it
affected a great many individuals here, and those events took on the
proportion of public calamities. According to our records, the colony
was more like purgatory—a department of the Lower Zones—than
the place of rest and learning it was supposed to be.

"The previous Governor was perhaps a little too tolerant; and, as
you can gather, indiscriminate kindness tends to cause a lack of discipline and eventually a collapse of order. Then, two centuries ago,
one of the Ministers of Divine Union urged the Governor to change
the situation, which had become deplorable. The Governor, with the
support of the Ministry, banned widespread communications with
Earth. There was enormous opposition, naturally; but the Minister
who had introduced the measure called the community to witness
Jesus's teaching, 'Let the dead bury their dead, and in a short time
the change was generally accepted."[16]

"Still," I insisted, "don't you think it would be comforting to hear
news about loved ones on Earth? Wouldn't we feel more at ease?"

Lisias had been standing by the screen all this time without turning it on, as if waiting to give a more complete lesson.

"Let's see if that would be so wise, "he said. "Take your case, for
example. Would you be prepared, say, to hear that your son, whom
you love so much, was harassing someone or being harassed himself? Could you maintain the necessary serenity if you knew that?
Would you act according to Divine principles, awaiting and keeping
faith? If someone told you that one of your brothers had just been
convicted of a crime and sent to prison, would you be strong enough
to keep calm?"

I had no answer, except for a weak smile of recognition.

"We shouldn't look for news from Earth," Lisias went on, "except
when we're able to actually help someone. We ought to remember,
too, that no one can give worthwhile help, and do it well, while suffering emotional or mental disturbance. We have to prepare ourselves before we renew direct contacts with relatives on Earth. Most

----

[16] *Translator's Note: Luke 9:60*

incarnates, unfortunately, haven't achieved even moderate self-con-trol. They lead haphazard lives, drifting with the high and low tides, depending on how materially well off they are. If our loved ones offered us a space of spirituality and tenderness then it would be dif-ferent. The point I want to stress is that no matter how we feel, we have to avoid being drawn into low vibratory states."

I still clung to my point. It was evidence of my continuing stub-bornness, I suppose.

"But Lisias," I said, "your father is back on Earth. Wouldn't you like to communicate with him?"

"Sure I would," he answered. "And whenever we deserve the joy, and the contact between us serves a beneficial purpose, we visit him in his new physical body. But we're fallible too, so we always refer the matter to the departments responsible for his new program on Earth and let them decide on the right opportunity and the merits of the case.

"This work," he continued, "is done by the Ministry of Communication. It's a matter of some delicacy. You see, we must consider the fact that although it's easier to move from a higher to a lower spiritual plane than the other way around, there are certain rules that must be observed. These rules tell us that before we can give proper help to someone in a physical plane, we must have a thorough understanding of the person's realities. In such cases, it's just as important to know how to listen as it is how to speak. This colony was once in a constant state of turmoil because individuals here didn't know how to listen, and therefore couldn't give effective help to anyone. As a result, the spiritual atmosphere around here was often distressing."

I could see that these were irrefutable arguments and fell silent. Meanwhile Lisias turned on the device under my watchful eye.

Chapter
Twenty-Four

A SOUL-STIRRING APPEAL

Soft music floated into the room, soothing in its melody and cadence. On the screen an announcer appeared, sitting in a studio-like setting.

"This is Station Two, coming to you from Residence,"[17] he began. "Our colony continues broadcasting appeals for peace on Earth. We urge all workers of goodwill to muster their energy and help maintain the planet's moral balance. We ask for help from anyone who can spare a few hours to cooperate in the border region between the Lower Zone and humanity's mental sphere. Groups of misguided and vicious individuals, having left a bloody trail of war in Asia, are now laying siege to Europe and inciting new crimes. Our colony, as well as everyone dedicated to the work of spiritual sanitation in the Lower Zone, denounce this onslaught of the powers of evil. We're requesting dedicated volunteers and all the help possible. Remember—the cause of peace needs defenders! Join in and cooperate with us in whatever way you can. There's work for everyone, from Earth to our very gates! May the Lord bless us!"

The announcer's voice went silent and again the divine melody filled the room. But the serious tone of the call had stirred my very soul. Lisias hastened to my aid with his usual explanations.

"We're watching a broadcasting station in Residence," he told me, realizing that I was struggling to understand what I'd just heard. "Residence is an old colony closely connected with the Lower Zone.

----

17 *Translator's Note: Residence: another spiritual colony near Earth.*

On Earth it's now August, 1939.[18] Of course, you've been going through a great deal lately and haven't had much time to think about how serious the situation has become there. But as we've just seen, Earth is facing the threat of an eminent and major war."

"What?" I asked, awed by the idea, "Wasn't there enough bloodshed in the last World War?"

Lisias looked at me in silence; a sad smile spread over his features as if he were grieving at the seriousness of the problem. It was the first time he had failed to answer one of my questions, rhetorical or not; his silence was strange and a little upsetting.

The extent of the spiritual services in my new plane of life both impressed and overwhelmed me. Were there, then, spiritual colonies where generous individuals asked for help and cooperation? The tone of voice of the announcer clearly indicated that he was putting out an S.O.S. His fatigue was easily visible on our screen, and his troubled eyes betrayed a deep anxiety. And what about his language? I had heard him express himself clearly and correctly in my own tongue, though I had taken for granted that all spiritual colonies communicated with each other telepathically. Were there, then, real problems in the communication arena?

Lisias saw the bewilderment on my face, and came to the rescue.

"We're still a long way from the ideally pure regions of the mind," he told me. "It's not as different from Earth as you might think. Spirits in perfect harmony with each other communicate through thoughts, without the limitations of speech. But in general, we can't do away with spoken language. Our stage of operations is immense. Humanity on Earth, numbering in the millions, is united with the planet's invisible humanity, now in the billions. But since it's impossible to reach the more perfect zones right after the death of the physical body, we don't necessarily possess such gifts of communication; so we keep our various national and linguistic heritages. In different sectors you'll find many individuals who are free from all limitations—but, in the laws of evolution, everything happens in

----

[18] *Translators's Note: These events took place as World War II was initiating in Europe. On September 1st, 1939, a few days after this conversation took place between Andy and Lisias, Poland was invaded by the German "Blitzkrieg"; on September 3rd, both England and France declared war on Germany. The book was dictated in the period 1942-43, and published in 1944.*

sequence. We just have to wait our turn."

As Lisias finished, the music on the imaging device stopped and the announcer returned.

"This is Residence, and you are watching Station Two," he said. "The colony continues broadcasting its appeal on behalf of world peace. At the moment stormy clouds are gathering over the skies of Europe. Destructive forces from the Lower Zone, attracted by some of humanity's most primitive instincts, are now spreading in every direction. At the same time spiritual benefactors are stationed in political offices around the globe, making great sacrifices in the continuing struggle for international harmony. Unfortunately, in some countries government power is too centralized, and opportunities for spiritual collaboration are few; a number of nations, lacking political bodies that would provide more calm and balanced political advice, are quickly moving toward a great and terrible war. Beloved spirits of the higher spheres, we must help preserve peace on Earth. Aid us in defending centuries of experience invested in the cultural and political centers of Western Civilization! May the Lord bless us."

Again the announcer's voice stopped, and music filled the room. Lisias didn't say a word, and I didn't dare speak. After five minutes, the announcer came back on.

"This is Residence, at Station Two. The colony continues asking for help in its bid to ensure peace on Earth. Fellow workers, brothers and sisters, together let's ask for the protection of the powerful Fraternities of Light which direct the destinies of America! Help us to preserve the intellectual heritage of humankind! We now need to hurry to the rescue of defenseless communities, and console the agonized hearts of countless mothers. Presently, our forces are concentrated on the tremendous fight against legions of ignorant spirits. Give us all the help you can provide! We're the invisible part of Earth's humanity, and many of us will soon be going back to the planet to correct past errors. Incarnate humanity is also our family. Let's unite, then, in a single thought of peace. The advance of darkness must be stopped with floods of light. We must ward off the blows of evil with the shield of kindness. Rivers of blood and tears threaten to flood the fields of Europe. We must commit ourselves to constructive work and the strengthening of faith. May the Lord bless us!"

The broadcast ended. Lisias turned off the imaging device; with a discreet movement of his hand he wiped away a tear he couldn't hold back. Then, turning to me, he said, "What devoted workers the brothers and sisters of Residence are. But," and here his voice grew sad indeed, "the effort is useless. Soon humanity on Earth will be facing tremendous carnage and suffering."

"But isn't there a chance of avoiding this madness?" I asked, greatly disturbed by what I'd just heard.

"Unfortunately," Lisias replied in a serious tone of voice, "the state of affairs is extremely critical. In answer to appeals from Residence and other colonies working near the Lower Zone, several conferences have been held here. But the Ministry of Divine Union has already warned us that war is inevitable.

"Humanity as a whole is like a compulsive eater who's gone to a banquet and gorged himself: the digestive trouble that follows can't be stopped. Several nations have been at an orgy of criminal pride, boastfulness, and murderous selfishness. Now they're faced with the need to get rid of these poisons as fast as possible."

I could see that he was anxious to drop the subject, all too painful to both of us, and softly suggested that we call it a night.

Chapter Twenty-Five

A GENEROUS INITIATIVE

E arly the next morning all of us shared a light meal. As her children were leaving for work in the Ministry of Assistance, Laura, to help me overcome any hesitation about the day, said cheerfully, "I've arranged some company for you today, Andy. I've asked Raphael to stop by and meet you. He's an old friend of ours who works at the Ministry of Renewal. He'll take you over there and introduce you to Minister Gentile at my recommendation."

This thoughtfulness on her part left me speechless. I positively beamed at her. Lisias, almost as pleased as I was, gave me a warm hug on leaving. Laura kissed her son goodbye—"And oh yes, Lisias," she called after him, "would you tell Minister Clarence that I'll come over as soon as Raphael comes for Andy?"

"Of course," Lisias answered cheerfully.

When we were alone again, Laura said in her usual kind way, "Andy, new paths are going to open up for you today. Since your mother doesn't live in Nosso Lar, do you mind my taking her place for a moment and offering you a little motherly advice?"

"I'd appreciate it very much," I replied. "I don't know how I'll ever be able to thank you for all your kindness to me."

Laura accepted this declaration with a smile.

"I heard that you asked for work some time ago," she began.

"Yes, yes, I did," I said, and thought of Clarence's words on the subject.

"I also know that you didn't get it then, but did obtain permission to visit different Ministries—at least the ones that connect us to Earth."

"Yes, that's right."

"That's what I'd like to talk to you about. I do have more experience in these matters—don't you agree?

"First, now that you're finally being allowed to visit different work departments in preparation for your apprenticeship, try not to ask questions just out of curiosity. Second, don't be like a moth fluttering from one candle flame to the next, going from one department and possible job to the next.

"Of course, I do appreciate that you have a strong intellectual bent. You're a brilliant physician, and have an inquisitive mind, so it wouldn't be hard in your present circumstances to start down the wrong path. Remember, there are more important and beneficial ways of learning than merely analyzing things. Sometimes even healthy curiosity can be inappropriate; however, those who are strong and willful can use it to get involved in all kinds of worthwhile endeavors. Remember, only the weak of character feel as if they are victims of indifference and rejection.

"Minister Clarence has given you a permit to visit the Ministries, beginning with Renewal. Very well; instead of trying to satisfy your curiosity, study the different kinds of activities as carefully as you can, and at the first chance you get, lend a helping hand if someone at the Ministry asks you to. Do it no matter how humble you think the service is. And while you're there, don't worry about the affairs of the other Ministries. Try to gain the trust of the individuals around you at Renewal—and keep in mind that the spirit of service should always have priority over the spirit of investigation.

"This goes not only for scientific curiosity but personal curiosity, too. Don't be a busybody. Second-guessing someone's actions without the proper credentials of good service could be seen as exceptionally rude. Not only that, but it could have an effect on you later: many failures on Earth start with this kind of kibitzing. Everyone's willing to be a spectator, Andy, but not too many actually accomplish something. The only thing that will merit your claim to new privileges is useful work.

"There's plenty of hard work in the Ministry of Renewal, because that's where the colony's lowest departments are. The individuals who are entrusted with the hardest missions are almost always recruited from Renewal's working staff. But please, Andy, let me stress again: keep in mind that the work there sometimes may be humble, but it's never demeaning. In all planes—from Earth to the highest spheres in the most spiritually evolved zones—the greatest worker is Master Jesus Himself, and He wasn't ashamed, remember, to handle a heavy saw in a carpenter's shop.

"Minister Clarence has given you a chance to learn, analyze, and appreciate these values. Be a wise worker; turn this observation period into a stage for doing some really worthwhile service. The individuals in charge might not let you adopt some special line of work because it may be reserved for those whose efforts and experience have qualified them for it; and there's no question that they're perfectly right to make those decisions. But, believe me, they'll look very favorably on the cooperation of someone with goodwill—someone who shows a real desire to serve and doesn't argue about the available positions."

Laura's words, all affection and motherly concern, were a balm to my heart. Very seldom had anyone expressed such a deep and loving concern about what happened to me. Her advice affected me more than I could have guessed, and I listened to it at times with tears in my eyes. Laura, seeing this, wanted to infuse the moment with an invitation to love.

"The ability to start over," she said, in an encouraging way, "is one of the greatest lessons we can learn. Not many understand it, and it's rare to find among the souls of Earth those who apply the lesson to themselves consistently. Recall, though, in the New Testament that there was once a learned member of the Sanhedrin—the hope of his people—who enjoyed an enviable position in Jerusalem. Then one day he abandoned everything and went into the desert to start his human journey over—as a simple weaver. His name was Paul of Tarsus."

I couldn't stop myself any longer. My eyes filled with tears, and I took Laura's hand in mine, more like a grateful son than the relative stranger I was. She seemed to look then beyond the room and into a place deep within her own heart.

"I'm grateful, too, Andy," she said gently. "I don't think you were brought into this house by a blind stroke of fate; we're all bound by ties of affection. I'll be going back to the physical plane soon. But in our hearts we'll continue to be united because of those ties. And I hope—I truly hope—to see you busy and happy before I leave. Just remember this house is your home. And if you want to demonstrate gratitude, do two things: work with goodwill and put your trust in God."

I looked into her kind face then and knew—for the first time, it seemed to me—the joy that comes from a purely spiritual friendship. It was as though I had known her as a devoted friend for a long time, but when I tried to place her in my earliest memories, I came up with a blank. I felt at that moment like hugging her again and again. But just then a knock rattled the door.

"That'll be Raphael coming for you," said Laura. She might have been a mother talking to her youngest child. "Go along now, Andy, and think of Jesus. Work hard for the well being of others—it's the only way of finding your own happiness."

Chapter
Twenty-Six

*N*EW PERSPECTIVES

*N*ot long afterwards, Raphael and I left. As we walked through the streets, I kept mulling over Laura's advice, suddenly realizing that I was about to begin not only a series of visits of study, but also a term of apprenticeship and service.

The district we were passing through on the way to meeting with Minister Gentile was imposing in its beauty, but my mind was elsewhere. I was not in my usual inquisitive frame of mind. Rather, I was experiencing a mental activity that was new to me: I was praying fervently. Once, long ago, I had been hostile to the idea of prayer, let alone the practice of it; now, to the same degree, I turned to it as the mainstay of my determination to serve. I asked Jesus to help me in these new circumstances, so that I could find work and the strength to do it.

I must, all this time, have been a puzzle to Raphael, whom I was following in silence, since from time to time he would give me a curious look, as if he hadn't expected such an attitude from me.

We eventually took a transport to the Ministry. It stopped in front of a large building, and we got off without so much as a word between us. In a few more minutes we were shown into the Minister's office. Minister Gentile, I discovered, was an older, good-natured man, with an expression and manner that showed him to be an individual of uncommon vitality.

Raphael introduced me as Andy, Laura's friend, and then took his leave, offering his respects to the Minister and an encouraging handshake to me. He was, he said, urgently expected at work.

After he'd left, Gentile turned his clear eyes toward me and said,

"Clarence has already mentioned you with interest. The Ministry of Assistance often sends groups of its members on observation visits to us. And as a rule, such visits turn into periods of service."

This allusion wasn't lost on me.

"That's exactly what I want most, sir" I replied. "I've asked God to help me and to let my stay in this Ministry become a period of apprenticeship as well."

These words seemed to move Gentile. A new feeling of reverence grew in me, and I decided to seize the moment.

"Minister Gentile," I said, "Right now, I understand, as I never have before, the urgency of redeeming myself. I've wasted so much time on foolishness, so much energy in ridiculous self-worship. But I also know that my coming here through the Ministry of Assistance was no accident: it was God's mercy, and may even have been an answer to my mother's intercessions. I also know that, until now, I've received many benefits without offering a single useful act in return. My growing conviction is that I belong here, where so much redemptive work takes place. So if possible, please let me turn my visit into an opportunity to serve."

I spoke with sincerity, and he noticed it—I could tell by the expression in his eyes. A change had undoubtedly come over me, and it must have showed. Days ago, when I had asked Clarence for work, what I wanted wasn't clear to me in the least. Certainly, I had requested work, but not out of a desire to serve. Neither had I realized then the value of time, nor learned to appreciate the blessing of a second chance. The truth was that I had really wanted to continue being what I had been until then—a proud and respected physician, a slave to the absurd claims of self, the master of my own narrow views. Now, after all I had seen and heard, and after realizing the responsibility each of God's children has in the infinite scheme of Creation, I had given voice to what was best in me. At last I was being sincere. I wasn't the least worried about the kind of work I was to do. I really was anxious to carry it out in the spirit of service.

Gentile looked at me questioningly. "Are you really the former doctor?" he asked.

"Yes, I am," I replied, almost in a whisper.

The Minister was silent for a while, as if trying, like Raphael, to adjust himself to an attitude he hadn't expected.

"Well, your resolutions are certainly praiseworthy," he said at last. "May the Lord help you stand by them."

Then, as if to give me new hope and raise my spirits, he said, "When the disciple is ready, the Father sends the master. It's the same with work. When you're willing to serve, the opportunities present themselves. In your case, Andy, Divine Providence has been generous. You're eager to serve, you understand your responsibility, and you accept your duty. That's an attitude that will help you do exactly what you want. In the physical plane all the applause goes to the person who makes a fortune or does an important job; the case is different here. To us, what matters is effort, understanding, humility of heart."

He must have sensed the strength of my feelings, then, because he added quickly, "It's quite possible for you to get work in this Ministry. For the time being, though, it would be wiser if you were to visit our various departments and see what goes on there— observe and study the different activities."

He turned to a communication device on his table, and spoke into it to someone in the next room.

"Tell Tobias I'd like to see him before he goes down to the Chambers of Rectification, please," he said.

A few minutes passed and into the office came a young man who had, I thought, a pleasant air about him.

"Toby," Gentile said, pointing at me, "this is a friend from the Ministry of Assistance who's here studying and observing. I'm sure that a visit to the Chambers of Rectification would be highly beneficial to him."

I offered Toby my hand, which he shook with a strong, forthright grip.

"At your service," he said.

"Take him with you, please," the Minister continued. "Andy wants to become thoroughly familiar with all of our different activities here. So if you will, see that he's given every possible opportunity."

"I'm on my way there now," said Toby obligingly, "if you'd like to come with me..."

I took my leave of the Minister then, and he gave me some further words of encouragement. Within a few minutes, I had followed Toby out of the building and together we walked along large city blocks.

From the outside, they impressed me as busy work centers. Toby must have seen the silent questions forming within me.

"These are the great factories of Nosso Lar," he said. "Over a hundred thousand individuals work here. They do everything from preparing juices to manufacturing woven goods and every other kind of commodity you can imagine. And, at the same time, mind you, they're working for their own rehabilitation. And their enlightenment," he added.

Not long afterward, we turned, at Toby's prompting, into an imposing building. Before us stretched long galleries filled with large numbers of workers. Back and forth, they hurried in the pursuit of tasks I couldn't begin to guess.

Soon thereafter we came to a huge stairway leading down to the lower floors.

"Let's go down," said Toby. He must have intuited my confusion because he added, "The Chambers of Rectification are located near the Lower Zone. That's because when they first arrive in Nosso Lar, most of these unfortunate individuals can't stand either light or open air."

Chapter Twenty-Seven

*W*ORK AT LAST

I doubt if anything could have prepared me for the scene I saw. The Chambers of Rectification resembled neither a field hospital nor a conventional nursing home, but rather a series of vast interconnected wards crowded with human forms. From every direction came the sound of voices—a mixture of groans, sobs, broken phrases spoken at random and in utter agony. Everywhere, there was evidence of a terrible spiritual misery: ash pale faces, bony hands, contorted features. Indeed, these sights and sounds upset me so much that I only held on to my strength by turning to my one recourse—prayer.

Toby, who remained undisturbed, calmly called for the senior nurse.

"Why are there so few assistants here today?" he asked. "What's going on?"

"Minister Flacus," she replied. "He sent word for most of them to accompany the Samaritans on rounds in the Lower Zone."[19]

"Well, then," Toby said decidedly, "we'll have to fill the gaps as best we can. There's no time to waste."

Just then, from a bed nearby an old man cried out. He clutched at the bed with one hand and, with the other, made odd waving signs.

"Brother Toby, Brother Toby!" he called. "Have mercy! Help! Help!

----

[19] *Translator's Note: Samaritans: A team of workers from Nosso Lar which visits the Lower Zone on missions of rescue. Their purpose is to seek the individuals who are ready to be helped out and receive treatment. Such individuals are often taken to treatment centers, such as the hospital in Nosso Lar, where they can then start the process of adapting to their new reality.*

I'm suffocating! I want to leave this place, to—to—to get out. It's a thousand times worse than death! Help! I need air—I want more—air!"

Toby walked into the ward, bent over the old man, and examined him carefully.

"Why is Mr. Rivera so much worse?" he asked the nurse.

"He's had one of his worst attacks," she told him. "Assistant Gonzalez thinks it's mostly due to a discharge of heavy, worrisome thoughts sent out by his incarnate relatives. He's still very weak; he doesn't have the mental strength to break away from his earthly ties. Poor old fellow—he just can't resist his relatives' influence."

Toby gently stroked the patient's forehead, and gave the nurse a concerned look. "Any other disturbances?" he asked.

"Early this morning," the nurse replied, "he rushed out of the ward, yelling that he was needed at home. Said he couldn't forget his wife and children; said it was cruel to keep him here, away from them. Lawrence and Herman tried to get him back into bed, but he fought them at every step. I figured it'd be better for him if I took away his energy and mobility, so I gave him a soothing magnetic treatment."

"You did the right thing," Toby agreed. "I'll see to it that something's done to lessen the influence of his family's feelings. They have to be given a few more worries so they'll leave Rivera in peace."

I looked at the patient intently, trying to gauge his emotional state. He appeared to be mentally deranged; evidently, he was totally unaware of what was being said about him. He called Toby mechanically, as children do when they know someone will protect them.

My attempt to sort out his situation caught my new instructor's attention. "The poor old fellow's in a nightmarish phase," Toby said. "His soul is still trapped in its own misfortunes, so he doesn't have much idea of what's happening. Human beings, Andy, reap exactly what they sow. Poor Rivera here has been the victim of a great many illusions."

I wanted to ask about the man's history and why he was suffering so much, but remembered Laura's advice on curiosity and held my tongue. Toby spoke to the old man kindly, with words of encouragement and hope. He promised that he would see to it that means would be found for improving his condition, but that for his own good he ought to calm down and take his confinement in bed patiently. Mr. Rivera trembled and looked ghastly pale, but smiled sadly at these words and thanked Toby with tears in his eyes.

Leaving the anxious Rivera still trembling under his sheets, we slowly made our way through long rows of well-kept beds. A stench filled the entire place—caused, as I later learned, either by thought patterns of patients still under the impression of physical death or under the control of base ideas.

As we continued on, Toby explained, "The wards we are now visiting are only for male patients...."

At this point a voice cried out from somewhere near by, "Toby, Toby, I'm parched...starving!"

"Help me, brother!" yelled a second man.

"For the love of God, I can't stand this any longer!" another screamed.

In the face of so much suffering, I was heart-sick.

"Toby," I said, unable to hold in my feelings any longer, "It's so terrible to see all these individuals in such misery and torment. Why does such a depressing place as this have to exist?"

"When you look at this scene," he replied, with a great deal of understanding in his voice, "try to see beyond the pain and devastation. Remember, Andy, these patients have just left the Lower Zone, where they were subject to all kinds of pitfalls as the result of self-neglect. Here in the ward, patients are not only cared for, they're also prepared for their future rehabilitation. We have to keep in mind that their suffering is of their own doing. A person's life is always centered where his or her heart is."

He paused—impervious, it seemed, to the clamor around us. Then he added, "They're cheaters of eternal life."

"What do you mean?" I asked, struck by this phrase.

"They expected material wealth to have the same value here in the spiritual plane as it did on Earth. They expected their sensual pleasures, their power, their snubbing of laws, their self-centeredness to cross the barriers of the grave and still be in force here. They saw this life as offering them new opportunities to indulge themselves. They were reckless merchants of sensation. They forgot to trade some of their material currency for spiritual currency. Whenever you travel to a foreign city, you are always careful to stock up on the currency of that country. But in their case, even though they knew a final trip to the spiritual regions was inevitable, they somehow failed to provide themselves with anything of spiritual value. So that is what we see at this end—the wealthy of earthly pleasures become paupers in the spiritual world."

It was all too true. Toby's words couldn't have made more sense. Walking among the patients, he gave comfort and hope whenever called upon. He led me into the next ward. Narcissa, the senior nurse, went before us.

I entered and found myself nearly reeling under a disheartening surprise inside. It was a ward of vast proportions. Here and there, on very low beds, lay thirty two men, all with contorted faces. The only sign of life they showed was their barely noticeable breathing.

"These individuals are severely distressed," Toby said, "and they're sleeping much more deeply than most of the other patients. We call them the negative believers; instead of accepting God, they were complete slaves to self on Earth. They didn't believe in life, action, or service. The only accomplishments that interested them were abuse, irresponsible sensuality, and eternal nihilism. They turned their earthly lives into a preparation for a long sleep, since they lacked any appreciation of good, of reverence for life and service; now there's nothing left for them but to sleep for years and years—and dream, too. Not dreams anyone would ever want. They only have nightmares—ghastly nightmares—and nothing can be done to stop them, for now."

This explanation horrified me. I looked in silence at Toby, who now began to lay hands on some of the patients and pray.[20] As soon as his treatment was complete on the first two patients, both started vomiting. From their mouths poured a thick, sticky black substance with an awful smell.

"They're throwing up poison," Toby said simply.

Narcissa was doing her best to keep the mess cleaned up, but by now many of the sleepers had started releasing the same poison.

----

[20] *Translator's Note: A procedure very similar to what is known as the 'lay on of hands' on Earth, and explained in greater detail in Chapter 5.*

Somehow, I got hold of cleaning materials and set out to help her. The nurse seemed grateful for the assistance, and Toby glanced at me expressing both satisfaction and gratitude.

The work went on throughout the rest of the day. It brought with it a blessed sense of fatigue. I realized that none of my friends back on Earth could possibly have appreciated the joy that I, once a proud doctor, felt as I started my self-education all over again by willingly performing the humblest of nursing tasks.

Chapter
Twenty-Eight

*O*N DUTY

A few minutes after that evening's collective prayer, Toby switched on the radio to listen to the Samaritan Report on work in the Lower Zone (worker patrols on such missions, I learned, communicate with their headquarters at regularly scheduled hours). By this time the effort of my long day had worn me out, but my heart was singing with joy. At last I had work to do, and instead of leaving me empty, my services had invigorated me like some mysterious tonic.

Soon after Toby had turned on the radio I heard a voice say with a tone of urgency :

"Samaritans to the Ministry of Renewal, Samaritans to the Ministry of Renewal—we've just finished a difficult job in one of the darker abysses. A large number of individuals have been freed. We've also rescued twenty-nine brothers and sisters from the spiritual shadows. Twenty-two are mentally disturbed; seven are in a state of complete emotional collapse. We're preparing transportation for them now, and expect to arrive at the Ministry soon after midnight. Please have everything ready."

Narcissa and Toby exchanged significant glances at this news.

"What do they mean?" I asked after the broadcast. "Why the collective transportation? Aren't they all spirits?"

"You forget, Andy, that you came to the Ministry of Assistance using a transport yourself," Toby replied—and then added with a smile, "yes, I know all about your arrival here. You have to keep in mind that the Lower Zone isn't much different from Earth; spirits are surrounded by heavy energy fields and can't always do as they'd like. Look at it this way—the ostrich and the swallow are both winged birds, but when it comes to flight, the resemblance stops. The ostrich can't get off the ground; the swallow is free to challenge the skies any time it wants."

It was an interesting analogy. But longer explanations would have to wait.

"It looks like we'll have a big group tonight," Toby said, turning to Narcissa. "We may as well start getting ready now."

"We're going to need more beds," she replied, with some anxiety in her voice.

"Don't worry about that," answered Toby emphatically. "Put the emotionally disturbed patients in Wing Seven. The weak ones will go to Ward Thirty-three."

He rested one hand on his forehead, trying to think his way out of the other dilemmas facing him.

"The problem of rooms we can take care of," he said, "it's the problem of emergency help that worries me. The night shift is going to be spread very thin. Our best workers are over at the Ministry of Communication helping other teams with assignments on Earth, and we can't count on those who've been out with the Samaritans because they'll be exhausted when they get back."

"I'll be happy to lend a hand," I volunteered, and quickly added, "at least in whatever way I can."

Toby looked at me with gratitude; it was a look that gladdened me.

"But have you really made up your mind to stay in the Chambers at night?" he asked. I could tell he was a little surprised by my offer.

"Aren't the others also staying?" I said. "I'm feeling strong and fit. Besides, I have to make up for lost time."

He smiled. "Well then, your cooperation is welcome. Narcissa and the current shift will stay on, naturally. And I'll send over Venantius and Sal; they're two of our most dependable workers. I can't stay tonight since I have another task to finish up elsewhere; but I'll leave a set of detailed instructions. And if anything unexpected turns up, you or one of the assistant nurses can certainly call me."

With these decisions out of the way, we started preparing the Chambers as fast as we could. Narcissa, along with five aides, stacked linens onto carts and readied the nursing supplies. Toby and

I moved beds and other pieces of furniture into Wing Seven and Ward Thirty-three. All the time I felt happy, euphoric, though I was boned-tired. I couldn't explain at the time what was happening to me—and in any case I had little time to try.

In Nosso Lar, in offices and workshops where people are willing to do their best and understand the value of a job well done, to serve others is the highest privilege. To be honest, the hour-bonus and any other immediate reward I could gain for my work were far from my mind. But the thought of my new position satisfied me a great deal. I would no longer be ashamed to face my mother, or any of my benefactors in the Ministry of Assistance.

Before leaving, Toby shook my hand.

"May the peace of Jesus be with all of you," he said. "I hope you have a good night and put in some profitable work time. You can leave tomorrow morning at eight o'clock. Usually, twelve hours is the most we can do, but these aren't usual circumstances."

I was, I told him, more than happy with this decision.

Later, as our patients started arriving, I, along with the other nurses and aides, did what we could for them. Among all of us, Narcissa impressed me the most: her kindness was spontaneous, and she cared for her patients in a soothing, motherly way. Her generosity fascinated me too, and I tried to come into closer contact with her. It was an easy enough task, and I soon found myself enjoying her conversation, which was simple but nonetheless instructive. She was a wonderful woman—a living book with devotion and wisdom written on every page.

"Tell me, Narcissa, have you been working here long?" I asked during one of our brief breaks.

"Yes, I've been in active service in the Chambers of Rectification for six years and a few months. Got three more years to go before I can fulfill my purpose."

I gave her a questioning look.

"I need an endorsement," she explained, picking up on my puzzlement.

"Endorsement? What do you mean?" I asked.

"I have to meet loved ones who're now reincarnated. We have to get together to work out our advancement. I made a lot of mistakes in the past, you know, and I was always begging the folks in charge here to let me go back to Earth and carry out my plans. Then one day someone suggested that I talk to Minister Veneranda here at Renewal. So I went to her, and what did she do? Why, she agreed to endorse my plans over at the Ministry of Assistance! But there was one hitch. I had to work here for ten years, correcting what she called 'certain unbalanced emotional attitudes.' At first I thought it was a tough condition and felt like turning her down. But I gradually saw that she was right. After all, she was just trying to help me, not herself. Well, I can't even begin to tell you how much I've profited by agreeing to that condition. I'm a lot more understanding, and even a bit more balanced now. And I figure I'll live out my next lifetime on Earth in a more dignified way, spiritually speaking."

I was about to tell her how amazing I found her story, when a patient in a nearby bed started calling, "Narcissa, Narcissa!" I let her go. After all, what right did I have to keep this devoted woman, a motherly presence to the patients, from her duties just to satisfy my curiosity?

Chapter
Twenty-Nine

*F*RANCIS'S VISION

*W*hile Narcissa was busy with her patient, I received a call from Laura (through the internal communication system), wondering about my whereabouts. I realized then that I had completely forgotten to tell her about my decision to take the night shift at the Chambers. I apologized for my thoughtlessness and filled her in on the situation. Even over the wire I could tell how delighted she was at the news:

"That's wonderful, child!" she said at the end of our brief conversation. "My only advice is to love your work. Fill your heart with the joy that comes from being really useful. It's the only way we can bring about everlasting improvement in ourselves. Now, just one more word: Remember, this house is your home." Those words encouraged and delighted me.

Shortly afterwards, I went back to the Chambers and found Narcissa struggling to calm down a young man. He seemed to be suffering from some serious mental disorder, and seeing him flail around, I tried to help her restrain him. At times the poor man tried to get out of bed and run; at others, he stared into empty space, seeing something neither Narcissa nor I could.

"Help me, for God's sake!" he cried, his voice alive with agony. "Help! I'm afraid… afraid!"

A look of panic passed over his face, and again he screamed as loud as he could: "Sister Narcissa, he's coming—the monster! I can feel the worms again! Here he is! Save me from him! Send him away—send him away!"

"Now, now, calm down, Francis," the nurse said to him softly.

"You'll be free from him; he'll leave you in a minute. But it's all up to you; you have to understand that. Look, here's what we'll do. You just pretend your mind is a sponge, a big one that's been soaked in vinegar. What you have to do is wring out that vinegar—get rid of it. Try to imagine that. This vinegar is sour and we don't want anything sour in your mind. I'll help you as much as I can. But listen to me: you have to do the hardest part yourself."

Narcissa's tender and reassuring words eased Francis's fear somewhat, and he soon showed he was willing to go along with his nurse's visualizations. After a few moments, he turned ghastly pale again, and started yelling as before.

"Nurse, listen to me—listen, please! He won't go away. He's come to torture me! Look there! Look!"

Looking at the spot on which the young man's eyes were fixed, Narcissa said," Yes, I see him, Francis—I see him. But now you've got to help me drive him away. I can't do it without you."

"Oh, it's a devil, that ghost!" he shouted, then wept like a child. I felt sorry for him.

"Put your trust in Jesus, my child," continued Narcissa in her soothing way "Think of Him, and forget the monster. I'm about to treat you magnetically. The ghost will go away."

She gave him a healing treatment, and almost immediately a calming, soothing energy seemed to fill him—I could see his expression change before my eyes. In a second or two, he looked up in a show of great relief and thanked Narcissa.

"I feel much better now," he told us.

Narcissa fluffed up his pillows, made him as comfortable as she could, and asked an aide to bring him a glass of magnetized water.[21] Throughout the event her example had been one of amazing inspiration to me. Her goodness was contagious.

She noticed that I was eager to learn about what I had seen, and was willing to initiate me into this secret of service to others.

"What was he talking about?" I asked, once we were out of

----

[21] *Translator's Note: Along the same principles that operate in the laying-on-of-hands technique, spiritual energy may be applied to the water. Water's properties, the spirits teach, make it a very effective carrier of subtle spiritual energies both at the physical level (i.e. Earth) and in spiritual planes where the spiritual body is still relatively dense.*

earshot of Francis, "Is some kind of shadow after him—one I can't see?"

"Oh, no," she answered. "He meant his own corpse."

"Corpse! How can that be?" Her response, I have to admit, shocked me.

"The poor boy was killed in an accident," she replied. "It was his own carelessness, but that's how he got to the spiritual sphere. He was young, and like many young people exceedingly fond of his body; so for days he wouldn't leave his grave. He refused to accept his new situation—which is nothing out of the ordinary. To tell you the truth, he was so deluded that he spent a long time trying to raise up his body, rigid as it was. The unknown scared him; he couldn't face it. And, of course, he wouldn't pay any attention to spirits from the higher spheres who were trying to help him. As far as he was concerned there was no such thing as eternal life—he'd set his mind against it.

"The decomposition finally did it." Narcissa continued calmly. "The decomposition hurt him so much that the poor thing ran away from his grave, just horrified. After that, he began his long wandering through the Lower Zone. And he might have stayed there longer than he did, but since the individuals who were his parents on Earth enjoy considerable credit over here, they interceded for him. That's how he came to be rescued by the Samaritans. They brought him here almost by force. I suspect he won't be leaving the Chambers of Rectification for quite some time—his condition is too serious. His father is in a difficult mission a long way from Nosso Lar."

"Has he been here to see Francis?"

"Yes, twice, and I'll tell you, his grief broke my heart. The boy's mind is in such bad shape he didn't even recognize his own father; he just kept crying and shouting and begging. It was a sight to see. The first time his father visited, he came with Minister Padova of Communication, and while the Minister was here the father bore up under his sorrow just fine. You see, he owed Francis's hospital stay to the Minister and didn't want to complain or break down in front of him. Well, they'd been talking for a while about Francis's spiritual state when the Minister got called away all of a sudden. Right after he'd gone, Francis's father apologized to me for the human gesture he was about to make. He knelt down by Francis's bed and took the boy's hands in his, holding on to 'em tight, like he was sending vital energies into him: something to soothe him and bring him to himself, if only just a little. Then he kissed Francis on the forehead, and started crying.

"By this time, I couldn't keep back my own tears, so I left. I can't say what happened afterwards, and never dared ask, but I've noticed that Francis has been getting better and better since that day. He isn't lost in his insane world all the time anymore—he just has an occasional attack, like the one you saw; and even the attacks are getting less and less frequent."

The story of Francis had touched me deeply. "Narcissa," I said, still wanting to understand what I had just witnessed, "how can the image of his corpse come after him?"

"Oh, Francis's visions are nothing but hallucinations," she explained. "Lots of spirits suffer from them after the body dies. Some individuals are very attached to their bodies, especially if they live their entire lives through it and for it. So, when it's time for them to join the spiritual world, they can't bring themselves to leave those bodies, even if they're only corpses. They can't accept the idea of spirituality, you see, so they fight hard to keep the physical body. But after a while the decomposition starts, and they're repelled, and go to the other extreme. The vision of their corpses comes to them, as in Francis's case—tormenting their very essence. The vision seems so real to them that they live in a constant state of crisis, which can go on for a long or a short time. A lot of them suffer in the worst possible ways you can imagine until the ghost-corpses they've created finally disappear."

Narcissa's words, spoken so directly and simply, shocked me.

"Well, thanks to the Heavenly Father," she went on, seeing the effect she had had on me, "I've learned a great deal in my years of service. And one of the most important things is this: most of our brothers and sisters in the physical world are deeply asleep where their spirituality is concerned. But we can't let it worry us to the point of hurting us—the process is natural, in its own way. A grub sticks to a tree-trunk or a piece of board, but one day the butterfly breaks through it and flies away. A seed is so small you can hardly see it, but one day it starts changing and in a few years it's turned into a giant oak. A flower dries up and its petals fall to the ground, but its sweet smell stays in the air. Those are lessons we ought to remember. Before being born, all expressions of life appear to be asleep."

Narcissa grew silent then and seemed to withdraw into her own thoughts. It was a moment of privacy I dared not interrupt.

Chapter Thirty

INHERITANCE AND EUTHANASIA

I hadn't yet gotten over my amazement at Francis's case when Sal entered the ward and said to Narcissa, "Our friend Pauline would like to see her father, who's in Wing Five. I thought I'd better check with you before letting her in because his condition is still so serious."

In her usual quiet and compassionate way, Narcissa said, "Bring her to me, will you please, Sal."

"Pauline's giving up all her free time so she can bring the different members of her family together, " she said. "It's quite a tricky job, if you knew that family. Anyway, she's got Minister Veneranda's permission to see her father whenever she needs to."

Sal hurried off, and Narcissa added, "Pauline's a devoted, dedicated daughter. You'll see."

In a minute or so, a young woman came toward us. She was a slender, lovely being, dressed in a light silk dress that shimmered as she walked. She reflected an angelic beauty I'd seldom seen in anyone. Her eyes, however, showed deep concern.

Narcissa politely introduced us, and apparently feeling I could be trusted, Pauline asked anxiously, "How's Father, Narcissa?"

"A little better," the nurse answered. "Still, he remains pretty upset —unbalanced."

"It's such a shame," Pauline continued, clutching her hands in frustration. "He just won't change his mental attitude, even a little, and neither will any of the others. They're all so stubborn, Narcissa. Always the same hate, always the same lack of understanding."

To this comment, Narcissa said nothing. Instead she asked us to follow her, and shortly we found ourselves standing beside the bed of what looked to be a highly disagreeable old man. A scowl of bitterness seemed to be permanently etched on the old fellow's features. Physically, he was a wreck. A mop of disheveled hair hung loosely from his head, set off by thin drawn lips and a road map of deep wrinkles. He inspired more pity than sympathy, I thought. But, as best as I could, I tried to control such insensitive ideas and see in him a spiritual brother. With the effort, my feelings of repulsion began to disappear somewhat, and my mind became clearer. After all, what had I looked like when I first arrived at the Ministry of Assistance? What a repellent thing I must have been, staring here and there with desperation written all over my face. Yes, this was a valuable lesson—a lesson in humility. I thought, "One should always consider people's imperfections in light of one's own"—and it struck me that this would be a good approach for most of us to take. As I began to find out from that moment, seeing other people's pain as we see ours always opens up room in our hearts for compassion and love.

Once beside her father, Pauline greeted him affectionately; but the old man didn't have a single loving word for her. Instead, he glowered—his eyes harsh and filled with a fierce anger. He looked into her face as if he were a caged animal.

"Are you feeling better today, Father?" asked Pauline. She spoke with loving respect.

"Better! No, I'm not better!" he spat out. "I can't get that rascal out of my mind. I don't have any peace here—not for a moment. I can still see him leaning over me, pouring deadly poison into me!"

"Please, Father, try to forget all that. Remember that Albert came into your home as a son, sent to us by God..."

Earnest as it was, this plea went nowhere.

"My son? Never!" bellowed the old man, "He's a common, low-down criminal. He doesn't deserve my forgiveness—and he won't get it, ever. My son? He's the son of the devil, that's what he is."

Tears welled up in Pauline's eyes at this outburst.

"Father, let's learn from Jesus," she said, speaking to him in a tone of quiet persuasion. "He told us to love one another, didn't He? Oh, I wish so much that you could understand: our family experiences on Earth are ways of teaching us about real spiritual love. Actually there's only one true Father, and that's God, Who's eternal; and He gives us the chance to be fathers and mothers so we can learn to love each other. Our families are really testing grounds where our feelings and thoughts are purified. They exist so we can learn to come together; they're our preparation for a future of universal solidarity and comprehension. Father, we have to struggle—yes, and suffer a great deal sometimes—before we can call each other brother and sister and have those words mean anything. The whole Creation is one big family, and it all moves and is held together through the loving care of the one Heavenly Father."

The old man, listening to this sweetness coming through his daughter's voice, broke now into convulsive sobs.

"Please forgive Albert!" she continued, "Don't just look at him as a wild son. Try to see him as a child who needs to be enlightened. Father, listen. I've just come from our home on Earth, and I can tell you that I saw serious problems there. Let me tell you something that may surprise you. As you lie here in your bed you're constantly projecting thought-waves of bitterness and anger to our family, even though they're on Earth; and they're doing the same thing to you. You're both working together to poison each other. Did you know that thoughts can do that, Father? Any thought is a wave: when it's directed outward, it never misses its target, no matter how far away it is. That's why you're suffering. You and our family are exchanging hate and suspicion, causing both emotional ruin and pain.

"Mother simply hasn't been able to take all the stress and tension at home," she said, trembling slightly. "And you have to know—she was admitted to a psychiatric hospital a few days ago. Amanda and Cassilda are suing Albert and Angelo. They want to get hold of as much of your money as they can. It's a sad situation, Father—the saddest one I can think of. But it would improve considerably if you did one thing—stop using your mind (and we all know what a strong mind you have) to plan your revenge. Look at what's happened to us all. Here you are in the spiritual world in a condition of absolute collapse. On Earth, Mother is so disturbed she can't function, and your children hate each other. And what's in the middle of it all? The money you left. What's the use of all that money, if it can't buy even a moment of happiness?"

"But I left enough money to keep them all comfortable for the rest of their lives," the old man protested. "I was always looking out for their welfare...."

"When it came to money—yes, you did," Pauline interrupted. "But, when it comes to finances, one doesn't always know if what one is doing is for the best. There's another kind of wealth you could have left, though, but didn't—a sense of moral tranquility and some standard of right and wrong. That would have been the best inheritance we could have had. If you'd prepared all of us to earn an honest living, you'd have given us real wealth.

"Most times, Father, we're out to make lots of money because we're proud and ambitious. We want to be above everybody else. So we start focusing all our attention on external things, and forget more important and longer lasting ones: worthwhile knowledge, tolerance, humbleness of heart, understanding. No, we'd rather try to bend other people to our will. We become interested in having power and forget about the work God gave us to do, as well as about cultivating our spirits. But none of us is born on Earth simply to make a fortune. That doesn't mean that we can't manage what God gives us intelligently and take our fair share from what we earn. We're expected to be good stewards. But being greedy and domineering isn't a definition of good stewardship, Father. It isn't honoring God.

"Stewardship requires thoughtful responsibility," Pauline continued, "and it was this unrealistic idea of it that ruined our family. To put a few more cents in your bank account you'd deny yourselves anything. In the meantime I tried hard to take care of my brothers' and sisters' spiritual and psychological needs. But I couldn't be both father and mother to them; I couldn't give them what they needed. So Amanda and Cassilda never learned anything useful; they wasted their precious time, and finally married a couple of gold-diggers who were only interested in their money. Angelo fell in with the wrong crowd and flunked out of school; Albert became a doctor but wasn't really interested in practicing medicine, except for the odd cases that excited his curiosity. That's what money did to them, Father; it came easily and spoiled them, and it's not surprising that all they've ever thought about is their inheritance. All their spiritual possibilities have been ruined. That's the tragedy!"

The old man, suddenly became highly agitated again. Terror came over him.

"Curse you, Albert!" he yelled out wildly. "Nothing but a criminal! Nothing but an ingrate! You murdered me! I was just going to change the provisions in my will, and you poisoned me!"

"Please, don't say these things... show your son some mercy. Forgive and forget all that."

He went on cursing and swearing at Albert. When Pauline tried to speak to him again, Narcissa gave her a warning glance and called over Sal to help the old man, since he was now in a crisis. Pauline, saying nothing, tried hard to keep from crying; she stood by her father, gently stroking his forehead.

After a few minutes the three of us—Pauline, Narcissa, and I—left the ward. I was shocked and troubled by what I had just seen. Pauline talked in private with Narcissa for awhile and then took her leave, thanking us both for our patience and kindness. She departed as she had come, but with a worried and saddened expression.

"These inheritance cases are usually pretty tricky, "said Narcissa, once we were alone. "It doesn't always happen, but nine times out of ten big inheritances cause big trouble for both the givers and the getters. This case is even more serious than usual, because of the euthanasia. They were all so anxious to get their hands on the old man's money that when he got sick and lingered on, it was more temptation than, at least, one of them could handle. That money has stirred up all kinds of conflicts and misunderstandings in that family. But this is the way it usually happens: greedy parents raise big-spending children. I visited Pauline's home with her the very day her brother Albert—who's a physician—decided to put his father out of his misery. He used what they call the 'easy death' on him. We tried our best to stop him, but didn't succeed. Albert was deep into some financial trouble, and it bothered him so much that he didn't hesitate to move his father's death a little closer. Now you see the result: they all hate one another and are driving each other crazy. Well, God created spirits and blissful regions. But some of us aren't satisfied until we change ourselves into devils. We insist on creating our own private hells."

Chapter Thirty-One

A HIDEOUS BEING

*I*t was nine o'clock at night, and we hadn't had a moment's rest except for brief periods when there had been problems to discuss. One patient begged for help; another needed magnetic treatment. On our way to treat two patients in Wing Eleven, I heard screams coming from a nearby ward. I would have headed in that direction, but Narcissa held me back.

"Please don't go in there," she warned, "It's where the sexually disturbed patients are kept. The sight of them would be too painful to see. Wait till you're ready for it."

I didn't press the point, but dozens of questions crowded into my mind. A new world was opening up to me, and I was enormously curious about it. But I also had to concentrate on Laura's warning not to be too nosy because it could distract me from my proper duties.

Soon after nine, an odd little man—he looked like an ordinary worker—came out from under the trees of the park that surrounded the Chambers (I learned later that he was one of the guards of the Chambers of Rectification).

"Hello, Justin. What's the problem?" asked Narcissa. "Do you have a message for me?"

"I've just come to tell you there's a woman begging for help near the big field gate," he said with anxiety in his voice. "Guess she must've escaped the notice of the guards at the main gate."

"Well, why didn't you help her?" Narcissa asked.

The guard shrugged his shoulders and looked at us blankly, "Regulations say I can't do it — she's got black spots all over her."

"Is that so!" Narcissa sounded as if this were worrisome news indeed.

"Yes, Nurse Narcissa."

"Then it's a very serious case."

My interest was now peaked considerably, and when Narcissa started toward the gate, I followed her; together, we walked for a sizable distance across the moonlit fields. The park was silent, its trees covering the open grounds and rustling occasionally in the breeze. We must have gone well over a mile before the gate finally came into view.

On the other side of it stood the pitiful figure of a woman pleading for mercy. She was squalid-looking, dressed in rags, and outright repulsive. Raw, open sores were visible on her legs, but judging from Narcissa's startled expression, I realized that she must have seen many more details than I.

"Children of God," the woman cried out when she saw us. "Please give me shelter. I'm so tired. Where is Paradise? Isn't this Paradise, the place where I yearned to enjoy peace?"

Her shaking, tearful voice filled me with compassion. But Narcissa, though I could see that she too was moved by the beggar's plight, whispered to me, "Can you see the black spots?"

"No, I can't."

"Your spiritual vision isn't trained enough for it yet," she returned. "If it were up to me, I'd let her in right now, but when dealing with individuals in her condition, I can't make the final decision. I have to check with the Head Guard on duty."

She went up to the poor woman, and said in a gentle voice, "Please, just wait here a few minutes."

We hurried back to the guardhouse, and there, for the first time, I came into contact with the Head Guard of the Chambers of Rectification. Narcissa introduced us and briefly outlined the problem .

"You were right to come to me," he said, "Let's go see her."

We were soon back at the gate. The Head Guard carefully examined the new arrival from the Lower Zone, and in a few minutes declared, "For the time being, we can't do anything for her. She's one of the most hideous beings I've ever come across. We have to leave her alone."

I was shocked at the guard's attitude. Wouldn't we be neglecting our Christian duty to walk away from this poor woman and think nothing more of it? Narcissa seemed to have the same thoughts and tried pleading with the Head Guard. "But Brother Paul," she said. "What harm could it possibly do to give the woman shelter in the Chambers?"

The Head Guard nodded toward the beggar, who was anxious and impatient.

"Letting her come in would be dereliction of duty, Narcissa," he said. He gave the woman a long glance. "Have you noticed anything besides the black spots?" he asked.

Narcissa shook her head negatively.

"Well, I have," he continued. "Count up the spots."

Narcissa examined the woman a second time, and shortly said, "Fifty-eight."

"That's right—fifty-eight. Those fifty-eight spots represent fifty-eight children killed at birth," Brother Paul explained patiently. "For every spot I see the mental image of a dead child. She killed some of them with sharp blows to the head; others she suffocated. She used to work as a midwife, and took advantage of inexperienced young women. People would send these young women to her—people who wanted to ease their own consciences—and she'd commit infanticide, all for money. Well, she's in a lot worse shape now than even the suicide cases. Worse than most murderers, too, leastways the ones whose situations present attenuating factors."

I recalled many cases in my own practice in which, in order to save the mother's life, the unborn child's had to be sacrificed.

Brother Paul seemed to realize what I was thinking, "Of course, I don't mean legitimate cases," he added, "where an infant's life absolutely has to be ended to save the mother—those are trials of a kind. I'm talking about the crime of killing individuals who have a right to live and are just about to start their journey on Earth."

Narcissa was too inherently fine a soul, however, not to give in to her feelings of compassion.

"But Brother Paul," she said, again interceding for the woman, "I was a great sinner myself in my last life. Please, let's bring her inside. I promise to make her my own special patient."

"Narcissa," he answered with sincerity, "we're all indebted individuals. But we've improved enough to accept our failings and work to make up for our errors. This isn't the case with this woman. For the time being all she wants is to create disturbances and confusion among our workers. She's still bound up in hypocrisy, and someone like that sends out destructive forces. Now, I ask you, what good would guarding this place be if we didn't keep out harmful influences like that? Let me give you a little proof," he added.

He smiled in a sad, knowing way, and went over to the woman.

"Sister," he said to her, "what do you want us to do? How can we cooperate with you?"

"Help, help . . ." she replied, with a weary expectancy.

"But we have to learn to accept our suffering," he reasoned. "It makes up for our errors on Earth. Answer me this: why did you put an end to the lives of so many helpless little infants? Infants who had God's permission to begin living a life that would redeem them?"

With these words she looked around with suspicion. The next moment, a hateful expression crossed her face.

"Who's accusing me of such horrors as that?" she shouted. "My conscience is clear, you idiot! I spent my whole life on Earth working for the well-being of expectant mothers. I was compassionate and devout, good and pure!"

"Sorry," said the Head Guard, "but the records of your thoughts and actions say otherwise. I believe, my friend, that you still have not experienced remorse. When you open your soul to God's blessings and acknowledge your own failings, you can come to us."

"You're a devil, a warlock!" she yelled in fury. "Satan's own follower—that's what you are! I'll never come back here again! I'm waiting for the heaven I was promised, and I intend to find it!"

The Head Guard replied then in a firm tone, "Well, you're in the wrong place, then. Perhaps you'd better go look somewhere else. Your heaven isn't here. This is a place of work, a convalescence hospital. The brothers and sisters here help patients back to health, but the patients know they're sick and are willing to work for their cure."

"I haven't asked you for any help or any remedy," she fired back angrily. "All I want is the Paradise my good works entitle me to."

She turned away from us and walked off, though not before shooting a look of hatred in our direction. Then, to our astonishment, she abandoned her guise of the wandering beggar. Before our eyes, she stood erect and walked down the road defiantly, her steps firm, her gait haughty.

Paul kept his eyes on the retreating figure for awhile; then, turning to us, he said, "Do you see how hideous she is? She has crime written all over her, but pleads innocence to all of it. She's evil without a doubt, but she calls herself good and pure. She suffers spiritually in the worst way, but she pretends to be peaceful inside. She's created a hell for herself, but pretends to be looking for heaven."

We listened to the Head Guard with respect and new admiration at his insightfulness.

"Things aren't always what they seem to be, good or bad," he said. "Divine Providence never gives up on anybody. She will find help somewhere else. But it would've been a sin against real compassion, and the job I perform here, if I had opened that gate for her."

Chapter
Thirty-Two

ℐEARNING ABOUT MINISTER VENERANDA

*S*till bathed in moonlight and marvelously still, the park exercised an unusual fascination for me. The big, shady trees, the bushes with their slowly waving branches filled me with admiration. As we walked, I asked Narcissa to tell me something about it.

"The park has certain paths which lead to the Lower Zone," she said, "but we also grow fruit trees and plants here—for juice production, mostly. Minister Veneranda has also set aside areas for cultural purposes.

"They're called the 'green halls.' They're large areas among the trees, created in various artistic designs. The Ministry of Renewal uses them for lectures. The Governor lectures at a particularly beautiful one whenever he comes. The other ones are used for visiting Ministers—and the students, of course.

"But, oh my," she enthused, "you should see the trees when they blossom! That happens a couple of times a year. They look like little towers, all so colorful and the most charming sight you ever saw. The park is always filled then. We come out and the sky is our roof, so we can enjoy the sun in the day and the stars at night."

Narcissa spoke with such affection that I couldn't help exclaiming, "These lecture halls must be marvelous!"

"They sure are," she agreed.

"How did it all come about?"

"It was forty years ago when Minister Veneranda first had the idea," she began. "It stirred up excitement all over the colony, and there was a campaign to build the first 'natural hall,' as it was called. They began building arboretums everywhere. The Ministries, including Divine Union, cooperated with Minister Veneranda in building them all over the Water Park. But the school arboretums are the most interesting ones—take a look sometime. And not one arboretum is like another—so different in shape and size. One of them—Minister Veneranda had it built over at the Educational Park of the Ministry of Education—is shaped like a star; the number of plants and flowers in it would take your breath away. It's so big five teachers can each teach a large class there at the same time. In the center, there's a kind of projection system, which sometimes will be used for five different activities at once. Her projects improved the whole city, because they created places that were practical and also filled with spiritual beauty."

"How are they furnished?" I asked. "Nothing like lecture halls on Earth, I imagine?"

"No, it's all different," replied Narcissa. "Minister Veneranda thought of the Gospel passages that describe Jesus's life on Earth, and she suggested that all the building material be taken straight from nature. So each hall has benches and chairs that are sculptured with material extracted from the ground and covered with soft, sweet-smelling grass. Each one has its own characteristic beauty. She got the idea of natural furnishings from Jesus's sermons on the beaches along the Sea of Tiberias.

"The halls need a great deal of care," I offered.

"Yes, but when you see how much they give back in the way of beauty, they're worth it."

For a moment we paused and looked at the stars twinkling over-head. Silence had never seemed so perfect. When Narcissa broke it and we started up again, she took up the topic of the park a second time.

"As I said, the most beautiful hall in our Ministry is saved for the Governor's lectures. Minister Veneranda heard that the Governor likes ancient Greek landscapes, so she had the hall decorated with small fresh water channels, graceful bridges, miniature lakes, and plenty of shade trees with seats underneath made from woven tree limbs. She also planted many kinds of flowers, so that different ones bloom every thirty days. Each month has a new color scheme, and the most beautiful of all is the one that blooms in December. It's in celebration of Christmas, when the colony is flooded with the highest thoughts of all our brothers and sisters on Earth and all their plans and dreams, too. And of course we send our hopes and reverence to the spheres above as a way of praising the Master of masters.

"The Governor comes here almost every Sunday. He stays for hours sometimes, talking to the Ministers of Renewal as well as the workers. He offers suggestions on how to improve things, checks the border lines with the Lower Zone, meets with us and receives our well wishes, comforts the patients. And every now and then, when he has time in the evening, he'll stay and listen to music or go to the presentations put on by the students in the schools. Actually, most of the visitors to Nosso Lar come to our Ministry just to see the Governor's hall. It seats over thirty thousand people."

Listening to Narcissa talk in this way gave me the sweetest sensations—half joy, half curiosity.

"Minister Veneranda's hall," she continued with enthusiasm, "is another sight to behold. We give it special care and attention. Naturally, we can never do enough for her—or repay her for all she's done for Nosso Lar. She's a true servant of God, that woman is. She is responsible for creating all kinds of measures to help the unfortunate. The government itself praises her service record. She has more working hours than anyone else in the colony, and is the most senior officer in the Ministry—or the government, for that matter. She has serviced Nosso Lar for over two hundred years. Amazing isn't?"

I couldn't contain my admiration.

"She must be very revered indeed, then!" I exclaimed.

"You're right about that. Minister Veneranda is one of the most highly evolved spirits in the colony. Let me give you some idea of what that means: the Ministry of Renewal is under the direction of eleven Ministers, including her; the other ten never make any final decisions on critical matters without consulting her first. On many occasions, the Governor himself has asked for her advice. And here's another thing: she's also the only individual in Nosso Lar, with the exception of the Governor, who's actually seen Jesus in the Radiant Spheres. Do you think she ever mentions the fact? Never. She avoids all mention of it. But here's another story. One day, about four years ago, Nosso Lar was getting ready to entertain the Fraternities of Light who guide the Christian destinies of America. They had come especially to pay their respects to Minister Veneranda and to present her with a Service Merit medal for completing one million consecutive hours of dedicated service with devotion, persistence, and self-sacrifice. She's the first individual in the colony to ever be awarded such an honor. But when they gave it to her, she only cried and kept still. Later she gave the medal to the town archives. She transferred the honor of it over to the colony as a group, and said she wasn't worthy of it. The Governor protested, but she asked that all the celebrations be cancelled. She's never breathed a word about it since."

"An incredible woman!" I said, "It's a wonder she doesn't live on some higher sphere."

"Oh, in her inner self, she does—on a plane much higher than ours. She only stays in Nosso Lar out of a feeling of love and self-sacrifice. From what I understand, she's been working for a thousand years to help a group of her loved ones on Earth. She's been waiting patiently."

"I'd love to get to know her." I said with real earnestness. "Is that possible?"

This sign of interest pleased Narcissa and she answered: "Tomorrow, after the evening prayers, she's coming to the hall to lecture on the power of thought. Try her then."

Chapter Thirty-Three

CURIOUS OBSERVATIONS

*J*ust before midnight, I went, on Narcissa's orders, to the Chambers' gates. The Samaritans were expected at any moment, and someone had to watch for their arrival to make sure that any last minute developments were promptly taken care of.

My walk to the gate, amid large and trusting trees, inspired a great many thoughts and emotions. Here and there, among the trees, I saw large trunks that reminded me of the great oaks on Earth, and leaves that brought to mind acacias and pines. Out in the clear open air and surrounded by these trees I felt a well-being I'd never known in the Chambers. Peace took me over, and I began to reminisce about the events that had taken place since my first meeting with Minister Clarence. For instance, I wondered which one was the illusion—life on Earth or in this colony? I wondered what had happened to Celia and the children, and why no one had told me anything about them, even though I'd been given a great many explanations about other things. My own mother had advised me to keep quiet about the matter, and had only talked vaguely about my family. It all seemed to point to my need to forget the problems of the flesh, to renew myself. Yet, looking deeper, I found that my need for my family was still alive and strong. I longed more than ever to see my wife, and feel my children's arms around my neck. Why was fate keeping us apart—making me into something like a castaway on a desert island? Castaway or survivor, I couldn't blame anyone but myself for the situation.

Also, now that I'd had a chance to see the inner harmony that came from the intense and constructive work in Nosso Lar, I wondered how I could have wasted so much time on nonsense while on Earth. It was true that I'd dearly loved my wife and cherished the children we'd had. Yet when I looked back on my conduct as a husband and father objectively, I realized how I'd failed to build anything solid and useful in the spirit of my family. Unfortunately, I was only realizing it long after it would do any good. It seemed to me that I had advanced along the road without preparing for the future, without seeding the field or protecting the fountain that quenched my thirst, so to speak, and therefore I couldn't really expect to be rewarded at arrival. Upon leaving the physical plane, I was faced with the horror of ignorance. I didn't know what had happened to my wife and children, who in a moment had been deprived of their sense of family stability and security. How were they coping with the problems of being a widow and orphans? Those were questions I couldn't answer.

These thoughts kept running through my mind with irritating insistence. Yet a light breeze seemed to whisper elevated ideas, as if trying to lift my mind to higher thoughts. No matter how much these questions nagged at me inwardly, I had to focus on the mission I had been sent to undertake. Finally I reached the gate and scanned the distance beyond the tilling fields. Everything was moonlight and serenity. The sky was peppered with stars, and around me I could see only peace and beauty. Awed, I spent a few minutes in contemplative prayer to the Creator of all things.

That mood abruptly changed. I suddenly saw two enormous shapes walking outside, moving away from the gate. They mystified me totally. They looked like men, but at the same time seemed to be made of some undescribable, semi-luminous substance. A strange-looking radiance projected out from their bodies, and there was a long thread of some sort connected to their upper forms. My impression was that these were ghosts, and I couldn't bear to look at them. My hair stood on end, and I ran back to the Chambers in terror.

To my astonishment, Narcissa could hardly keep from laughing when she learned what had upset me.

"Well, now," she said, good-humoredly, "didn't you recognize those forms?"

I was feeling pretty sheepish by this time and didn't know what to say.

"I had the same experience as you, and I was just as surprised," she told me. "But it's not hard to explain. These figures are our own friends from Earth. Only they're highly evolved spirits living in the flesh, where they carry out elevated programs. Spirits like them, true servants of Eternal Wisdom, sometimes temporarily leave their bodies and travel through our spheres.[22] The threads you saw are just features that make them different from us, so you don't have to be afraid. Anyone who can reach as far as Nosso Lar is a very advanced spirit, even if they are unknown or humble on Earth. Let's go out and see," she added, giving me a bit of encouragement. "It's 12:40. The Samaritans won't be long now."

Narcissa's explanation calmed me, and I followed her back to the gate. I could still see the two figures in the distance, moving away from Nosso Lar.

"They're surrounded by blue light," Narcissa said, gazing at them. "Yes, no doubt about it: they are two spiritually advanced friends from Earth. I wish I knew what they're doing here, but they've come on a mission we can't know anything about."

We stood at the gate for some time, lost in admiration and contemplation of the silent fields beyond. Finally, Narcissa pointed out a dark spot traveling across the moonlit horizon. "They're here," she said. I looked in the direction she was pointing and saw a caravan moving slowly toward us under the clear sky. All of a sudden I heard barking sounds in the distance.

"What's that noise?" I asked, startled.

"Why, dogs," came the reply. "Dogs are valuable helpers in the Lower Zone, Andy. There are some dense, dark parts in the Zone, and it's not only discarnates who walk there but really scary individuals that I won't describe right now. I'll tell you about them sometime." At this, she called out to one of the aides who had followed after us, sending him back to the Chambers with the news that the Samaritans had arrived.

The group now approaching us was, to say the least, odd. Six big carts, drawn by animals that even at a distance looked like mules,

----

22 *Translator's Note: This is what metaphysical and parapsychology literature ordinarily label an OBE, Out-of-Body experience. The cord is known as the silver cord. It is the bond that keeps the spirit connected to the physical body throughout earthly life.*

lumbered along, preceded by lively packs of dogs. Most interesting of all was the flock of large birds that flew close to the carts making strange cawing sounds.

"What about our buses?" I asked Narcissa. "Can't they be used in the Lower Zone?"

She shook her head. "It's a problem of density," she said. "Not all matter has the same consistency. Take water and air, for example. An airplane can fly through the air but not under water. It's the same here. Of course, we could build machines that would carry us through heavier matter—you know, something like an earthly underwater craft—but the community prefers to provide transportation from the Lower Zone in this fashion. Besides, we can't do without animal cooperation at times."

"Animal cooperation?" I asked. "Why do you need animals?"

"Dogs make the work simpler. The mules can carry a lot of weight and are very patient. They even help warm the patients and Samaritans if it becomes necessary. And the birds," she added, pointing up at them, "are called 'traveling ibises.' They are important allies for the Samaritans. They destroy hateful and evil thought forms that exist in the more troubled regions in the Lower Zone."

The caravan was almost on top of us now.

"Well, I wish we could keep on chatting like this," said Narcissa in a kind manner, "but they're almost here. You ought to go visit the parks of instruction and the laboratories over at the Ministry of Education. There you'll find out more about animals."

Without another word, she began supervising her team of aides and doing last-minute work that was needed to receive our new patients.

Chapter
Thirty-Four

*N*EWCOMERS FROM THE LOWER ZONE

he packs of dogs, leashed and under the control of a few of the heftier workers, stopped as soon as they got to the gate. Within minutes, we were all making our way through the broad halls that lead into the Chambers of Rectification. Aides hurried about. The weaker patients were helped indoors. Along with Narcissa, Sal and other workers, the Samaritans did whatever they could, eager to help the newcomers, some of whom waited their turn without complaining while others griped and fussed noisily.

I also lent a hand. At one point I noticed an old lady trying with considerable difficulty to climb out of the last cart. She saw me looking at her and pleaded, "Please, son, help me get down."

I turned in her direction. As I approached her, she made the sign of the cross.

"Good heavens," she said, "thanks to Divine Providence I've escaped purgatory. You wouldn't believe the devils they have there—and how they tortured me! It's a hellish, hellish place. But at last angels have come to my rescue."

For the first time I was hearing references to hell and purgatory from someone who at first glance seemed calm and reasonable. I helped her down, and, feeding my malicious curiosity, asked, "So, are you coming from far away?"

Just as I had with my own patients on Earth, I made a show of being greatly concerned, when in fact I was only satisfying my personal curiosity. Laura's warning on this score had slipped my mind.

The woman, seeing my interest, began telling her story.

"Very far," she said. "On Earth, I was known for giving to charity, for being religious and very sincere in my beliefs. But what can one do against the snares of Satan? The moment I left the world I found myself surrounded by hellish beings — hellish, I tell you! They dragged me along with them so fast it was like being in a whirlwind. At first I asked the Celestial Archangels for help—the monsters kept me prisoner anyway. But I never lost hope. Not once. I knew I could be rescued at any moment because I'd left money to have monthly masses celebrated for my eternal soul."

I fell back now into my old bad habit of intruding into matters that were none of my business.

"That's very interesting" I said. "Didn't you try to find out why you were kept so long in that horrible place?"

"Absolutely not," she replied, and crossed herself again. "As I said, I always did my best to be good and devout on Earth. But nobody is completely without sin, are they? And my sins weren't altogether my fault. I was a rich woman and I might have led a peaceful life. But I owned slaves, and they were always getting into mischief and quarreling with each other. So they had to be punished when it was necessary; and that was all too often. Naturally, I had to be firm when I gave my orders, making sure my overseer carried them out to the letter. What I learned over time was that sometimes you had to make an example of one of these people. But in setting an example, you often lost one of them at the whipping post. That was unfortunate, I'll have to say. I lost property and the slave lost his life—but you can't always control these things. Oh yes—I occasionally had to sell female slaves just to keep trouble from stirring up. It separated them from their children, I know; but it had to be done. And I don't mind telling you that my conscience stung me a good deal when those things happened. But every month Father Amancio would visit the plantation and I'd confess. He'd give me absolution, then I'd receive communion, and then I'd be free from all those venial sins, at peace with God and the whole world."

Those easily spoken words shocked me.

"But my friend," I said, trying to reason with her, "that kind of peace is false. Don't you know that slaves are our brothers and sisters, and that to God the child of a slave is just as good as the child of a master?"

"God forbid!" She stamped her foot in angry protest. "That can't

be! Slaves are slaves, or the Church would teach us differently. Why,
there are slaves at the bishop's house, so why shouldn't there be
slaves on our plantation? Who'd work the land if the blacks weren't
there to do it? Believe me, I did them a favor by letting them live in
my slave quarters. On my plantation, blacks never came near the
guests' courtyard except to carry out my orders. Father Amancio
once told me at confession that Africans are souless creatures; the
only reason they're born is to serve God in bondage. So why should
I have any scruples about dealing with them? I know them, and I can
tell you they're the devil's own children! I sometimes admired my
own patience in putting up with them. I can tell you in all honesty
that I passed over very suddenly from shock when the Princess's
decree abolishing slavery was announced.[23] Just think of it, letting
those scoundrels go free! It all happened long ago, but I remember it
perfectly. I'd been ill for a few days when Father Amancio came from
town with the terrible news. It was a blow, and from then on I began
to get worse. How could we go on living with those hooligans at
large? Of course, they'd want us to pay them back by making us
serve them. That's when I said to myself... I'd rather die than serve
creatures like that. I remember I had a hard time making my confession that day, and when it was over Father Amancio absolved and
tried to comfort me. But it didn't do much good. And what a time I
had with them once I passed over! It seems that all the devils in the
place are Africans, and they've been spying on me all the time. I've
had to put up with their presence constantly until today."

"When exactly did you pass?"

"May, 1888."

Heavens! I looked at her in amazement. She in turn gazed at the
horizon with dim eyes and said, "Naturally, it's quite possible that
my nephews forgot to pay for the masses, even though I made that
provision very clear in my will."

I was about to talk to her about brotherhood and faith, and tell her
a few things I felt sure would be new to her, when Narcissa stopped
by and drew me aside.

"Listen, Andy," she said in the kindest possible voice, "we're sup-

----

[23] *Translator's Note: In Brazil, where this woman lived during the late nineteenth century, slavery
was abolished in 1888 through a decree signed by Princess Isabel.*

posed to be helping patients and taking care of the emotionally disturbed right now. You seem to have forgotten that, dear. What good is all this information going to do you? Disturbed people will talk your ear off; if you listen to them you're throwing away your concentration, showing that you're no more balanced than they are."

She said those words in a tone so sympathetic they made me feel ashamed. I tried to find words for an apology, but was unsuccessful.

"Don't worry about it, Andy," she went on in a new, brighter tone. "Now, let's see to these disturbed brothers and sisters here."

"Does that include me?" asked the old woman who had overheard Narcissa and was clearly upset that anyone would suggest that she was in any way "disturbed."

"Of course not, dearie!" Narcissa, an instinctive psychologist, protested. "I didn't mean you at all. But I think you must be awfully tired after such a long stay in that dreadful place."

"Oh, more tired than you could ever imagine," the newcomer agreed. "You have no idea how much I've suffered, and how those devils tormented me..."

We could see that she was about to begin the whole story again, but Narcissa cut her off politely—giving me a subtle lesson.

"You shouldn't think so much about sad things, dear" she said. "I know all about the suffering you went through. But for the time being, just relax and let me take care of you."

She turned to an aide, and said, "Zachery—would you please go to the Women's Department and ask Naomi to prepare a bed for our new friend? We must get her ready for treatment."

Chapter
Thirty-Five

AN UNEXPECTED MEETING

A few of us were busy putting away the patrol gear and tending to the animals when I suddenly heard a familiar and very friendly-sounding voice:

"Why hello, Andy. Fancy meeting you here! This is a real surprise."

I turned around and saw, standing before me, a Samaritan I recognized. He was an old acquaintance of our family on Earth. I looked closer still; yes, there was no doubt about it: this was old man Silva. My father, the ever inflexible businessman, had once reduced this man to ruin. I wanted to return Silva's greeting, respond to his friendly approach, but my embarrassment overwhelmed me and I was speechless. Worse still, I had no way of hiding what I felt. In this new environment, the face reflects with absolute accuracy a person's true emotional state. Pretending was out of the question. Finally, Silva himself noticed how uncomfortable I was and came to my rescue.

"I didn't know you'd come here," he said, amiable as ever. "I had no idea I'd meet you in Nosso Lar."

With this second and apparently spontaneous expression of kindness I was finally able to shake hands with the man and mumble a few words. In my heart of hearts, I wanted to offer an explanation for our past attitude toward him—but the right words wouldn't come. My father's actions had forced this poor man into bankruptcy. How could there be any apology for that? Seeing him standing there brought everything back to me. It was like watching a movie. I could hear the tears in his wife's voice as she tried to explain that her husband had been ill for months; making matters worse, two of their children had gotten sick, too. Their expenses had risen far beyond their ability to pay; the medical bills had eaten up every penny Silva had saved. I remembered how that poor woman cried and begged for a postponement of her husband's debts. She had spoken humbly, turning every now and then to my mother as if hoping to find some sympathy and help in another woman. My mother, in turn, had pleaded with Father to forget the contract he'd signed, and not to pursue any legal action. But Father was used to successful transactions on a large scale and couldn't understand the retailer's problems. He was adamant. He was sorry about his client's bad luck, he declared, and would help him as he could, but there was nothing he could do but press the lawsuit. Doing so in these matters had been a long-established regulation of his firm, and he wouldn't think of breaking it. To the woman, he only offered the consolation that some of his other clients were in much worse shape even than Silva.

I recalled Mother's sympathy for Silva's wife as she left, still crying. It had been sympathy lost on my father, who remained unmoved by the suffering he'd just seen. Instead he had scolded my mother and told her never to interfere in a business matter again. After that, there was nothing left for the Silva family but utter financial ruin. Facing Silva now, I could still see his daughter's piano being carted away to satisfy his implacable creditor's claims. I can see it still.

Silva, lowly and penniless, had later moved with his wife and children to a small town, where undoubtedly they had led a life of hard work and poverty. That was the last I ever heard of the family—which, I thought, would hate us.

I was anxious to find some pardon for all of the difficulties this man and his loved ones had undergone, especially since Father had not been the only one at fault. I carried my own guilt in the matter. I had encouraged my father's attitude toward the Silvas and had thought that Mother, in all her mercy, was being a sentimentalist. I was still very young then, of course, full of myself and brimming with arrogance. The needs and sufferings of other people had scarcely touched me. I cared only about our rights. Despite my mother's urgings toward a better course, I was determined to hold to my position.

All of these thoughts and images sped through my mind as I

stood there with Silva. In one short moment I had crossed over into the shadows of the past, and now there was no holding back the pain I felt about the whole sorry affair. Silva's voice finally called me back to reality:

"Tell me, Andy, have you visited your 'old man'?"

The question rang with tenderness, freely offered, and it only increased my confusion. No, not yet, I answered, although I wanted to very badly—I just hadn't had the chance yet. Silva sensed the constraint in this reply, and realizing that he was causing me pain—though quite unintentionally—he started to leave. He patted me affectionately on the back and, saying nothing, went on his way. Bewildered and disconcerted, I went over to where Narcissa was working and told her about this unexpected meeting and the way we had met and parted on Earth. "What should I do now?" I asked her.

"Don't be too surprised," she answered. "Why, not long ago I found myself in the same situation. I've already met here several of the people I offended on Earth. I see now that it's one of God's great blessings. These encounters provide a new chance for us to take up friendships that were interrupted, and to fix the ties that were broken. Did you take advantage of this great opportunity?"

"What do you mean?" I asked her.

"Did you ask Silva to forgive you? Remember this: it's always a satisfaction to recognize your own faults. By now, you understand enough to be your own judge. If you admit to offending him, don't bypass this chance to make a friend. Go find Silva, dear, and tell him, openly, how you feel. He's a busy person—you may not get another chance for a while."

I hesitated.

"Aw, don't be afraid, Andy," she added. "Anytime we follow our mind and heart in doing what is good, Jesus gives us the help we need to overcome anything. Come on, take the first step! Doing what's right is a great honor—remember the lessons from the Gospel. Go out and find Silva, and make up with him."

These words set me in motion. I ran after Silva, caught up with him, and opened up my heart as I begged him to forgive both my father and myself for treating him as we did.

"Both of us were blind to everything but self-interest, Silva. We were interested in money, and we were presumptuous. When those two things go together it's easy to go down the wrong road."

Silva was, I could see, moved by this confession. Halfway through it, he cut me short.

"Listen, Andy, nobody's perfect. Do you think my life was blameless? Besides, your father was a real teacher to me. My children and I owe him a lot—he taught us about the great value of individual effort. Would we have made any spiritual progress if he hadn't decided to defend his rights? Over here our old concepts of life change, and we come to see that our supposed enemies are often the people who help us out most. Don't torment yourself over what happened to us. Instead, let's work with the Lord, and be thankful for the eternity of life."

He saw the tears in my eyes, and patted me on the back in a fatherly way.

"Now, don't waste any time over this," he added. "I hope to have the pleasure of visiting your father with you soon."

We shook hands in silence, and a new joy rose up in my soul.

A dark little corner of my heart had suddenly been flooded by a divine light—forever.

Chapter Thirty-Six

*T*HE DREAM

*O*ur work went on, uninterrupted. Some of the sick needed emergency care; the seriously disturbed, all the attention we could give them. By evening I'd mastered the technique of giving hands-on magnetic treatments, and used them on many of the patients. In the morning Toby returned to the Chambers; and, more out of his own generosity than any value in me, he praised my work in high terms.

"Well done, Andy!" he said with an encouraging handshake. "I'm going to mention you specifically to Minister Gentile and see that you get double hour-bonuses for your efforts."

I was about to thank him for his trouble when, to my surprise, we saw Laura and Lisias coming toward us. The three of us exchanged warm hugs.

"We simply had to come and tell you in person how happy we all are," Laura said, her face beaming. "I followed you in spirit through the night, and your first steps on the road of cooperation are a great joy to us. I had the pleasure of breaking the good news to Minister Clarence earlier this morning. He sends you his best wishes."

We talked for a while, and they wanted to hear all about my first day of service and what I had thought of it. I gladly told them. They asked if I'd like to come back home with them for a little rest afterwards; but Toby had already offered me a room near the Chambers where I could relax and sleep without bothering with the trip home, and I'd taken him up on it.

An urgent need to sleep now overcame me. What I didn't know was that the greatest joy of the day was still to come.

My room in the Chambers was large and comfortable, and Narcissa had made the bed for me. Alone I prayed to the Lord of all Creation, and thanked Him for letting me be useful at last and giving me such joy in it. Not long after, the "blessed fatigue" of the hard worker left me little time for other thoughts.

Within a few minutes of falling asleep, I felt a sensation of lightness throughout my body.[24] It seemed to me that I was being carried away on a small boat, sailing to a place I'd never been to or heard of. I couldn't tell where I was going. Beside me at the helm sat a silent man I didn't recognize, but it made little difference. I felt like a boy passing through wonders I had no way of describing, and lacking any desire to do so. The scenery was magnificent. It produced such an ecstasy in me that I let myself be carried along without a word, aware only that the boat seemed to be moving quickly, and at the same time gradually climbing upward. Soon, I found myself in a marvelous harbor and heard a voice calling me lovingly from the pier.

"Andy, Andy—"

I would have recognized that voice in the middle of a thousand others. It filled me with joy, and I scrambled out of the boat as excited as a child.

A moment later I was in my mother's arms.

She led me into a strange and beautiful forest—a place unlike any I had ever seen. The flowers along the path possessed a peculiar characteristic—they seemed to retain light, revealing fantastic patterns of colors and unforgettable perfumes. Around us stood great trees, beneath which shining golden flower carpets stretched out in every direction. Here an inexpressible sensation of peace and happiness took hold, different from any dream state I'd ever experienced on Earth. I had left my heavier body back in the room at the Chambers of Rectification—of that I was aware—and was now in a higher plane. My sense of time and space, however, remained sharp, and I felt my many emotions at that moment growing ever more

----

[24] *Translators' Note: The mind (consciousness), during the state of rest, can separate itself temporarily from the spiritual body. The process is in all respects similar to spiritual dreaming, or an Out-of-Body experience in the flesh. This process is likely typical between planes with a great difference in vibratory ranges.*

intense.

My mother gave me sacred words of encouragement, filling me with new confidence.

"I prayed to Jesus that you'd be allowed to visit me on your first day of useful service," she said. "Work is a divine tonic for the heart, isn't it, Andy? I've seen so many individuals, when they leave Earth, just waiting around without doing anything. They look for miracles that never happen; they reduce their chances to do any good by acting more like parasites. They'll talk about how their loneliness discourages them or how unfit they are to do the work the Lord called them to. But it's essential, Andy, that we take every chance we get in our lives to remember and serve God.

"Try to see it like this," she continued. "On Earth we might give a bowl of soup to a hungry man, medicine to the ill, sympathy to someone who's grieving. Actions like that are remembered forever in the House of God. In the spiritual world, the same thing is accomplished by giving an understanding look to someone who is guilty, sharing the word of the Lord with the despairing, communicating hope to one who suffers. These things are the blessings of spiritual work, and they're a credit of love in our favor."

My mother's face had never seemed so beautiful as when she said these words. Her eyes sparkled with a spiritual brightness; her hands irradiated enlivening energy and an indescribable sensation of bliss to me.

"In the Gospel, Andy," she went on, "Jesus tells us that giving is a greater joy than receiving. To be happy, you have to put that principle into practice on a daily basis. Always give, Andy, and above all give of yourself. Give in a spirit of tolerance, compassionate love, divine understanding. Material giving is a pathway for spiritual giving. Jesus gave more of Himself to teach humanity than all of Earth's philanthropists put together. Don't be ashamed to help the sick; don't be afraid to comfort the mentally disturbed patients in the Chambers of Rectification. Did you know that I followed your work there last night in spirit?

"Do all the good you can, Andy," she said with a smile. "But a word in your ear. In all our colonies you'll see individuals who are only looking for entertainment and anything new or faddish. Stay away from those distractions. Devote yourself to useful service. Remember that, as insignificant as I am, I can see, in spirit, your work in Nosso Lar, and at the same time follow your father's suffering in the Lower Zone. So just imagine how much God must be aware of. He sees and walks with all of us, from the most advanced messenger down to the lowest being in Creation. Nothing we do is hidden from God."

Mother stopped for a moment. By this time my eyes were so filled with tears, my emotions so deep, I couldn't say a word. She understood my feelings, and looked at me with warmth and affection.

"And here's something else to consider," she continued. "In most of our colonies, payment for work comes in the form of hour-bonuses. The hour-bonus brings two elements together. On the one hand, it means the possibility of receiving something from our fellow workers; on the other, we can use it to reward someone who's important to us. But how much value that hour really has is up to God alone. Now, we can make errors in rewarding hour-bonuses because we're evolving beings and still fallible. Which is why the real estimate of the hour is a private matter between the worker and the Divine Forces of Creation. It's also why our experiments on the road to progress—starting with the physical world—are always changing.

"The Lord, Andy, has administrators who've been given a chance to cooperate in the Divine Plan; they use tables and computerized registers, and they dispense payments. It's a temporary privilege, like the privilege of being fathers and mothers on Earth, or elsewhere for that matter. Conscientious administrators try to do their work to the best of their ability just as any parent who really understands his or her responsibilities is full of devotion and love. God, Andy, is both a careful administrator and a loving Father, never forgetting a single child. So the right to a direct understanding with each worker about the real value of his or her time is one which belongs only to God.

"When God rewards us in an outward way, it's only the transitory personality that's affected. But the real value of time is related to the essential being, the one that marches upward toward God's Glory. That's the reason God gives wisdom to those who spend time learning, and long-lasting vitality and joy to those who can forget themselves and serve others."

With these words Mother became quiet, giving me time to dry my eyes. She put her arms around me; and like a boy who falls asleep over his schoolbook, I lost consciousness of everything until, with a heightened sense of joy, I woke up in my room near the Chambers of Rectification.

Chapter
Thirty-Seven

*M*INISTER VENERANDA'S LECTURE

*A*ll through the next day, I found myself looking forward to Minister Veneranda's lecture—which was scheduled to take place, I discovered, after the evening service. Since I needed permission to go, I hunted up Toby.

"These lectures are only attended by really serious individuals," he said, looking very serious himself. "The instructors can't afford to waste time. But there will be hundreds of workers and patients from the Ministries of Renewal and Assistance there, so you might as well go along with them. And I hope you'll find it very worthwhile," he added with a smile.

I spent the day in intense activity. The visit to my mother and her talk on the practice of good had brought me considerable satisfaction—though her explanation of how the hour-bonus worked had raised some questions in my mind. Why, for instance, would God be involved in hour-bonuses? After all, wasn't determining someone's working hours an administrator's job? Here Toby came to the rescue. The administrator, he explained, was given the job of recording the periods of service and fixing standards and privileges as the worker earned them. Only Divine Forces, however, could accurately calculate the essential value of the time devoted to work.

"You know," Toby continued, "some workers will devote forty years to an activity and end up just as inept at it as when they began. That means they performed the task without dedication, without real interest. There are some people who live to be a hundred on Earth and leave it just as ignorant as when they came.

"To understand how exact your mother's explanation of hour-bonuses is, you only have to compare the hours spent by well-intentioned people to those wasted by wrongdoing ones. The well-intentioned are a blessing to others; the wrongdoers turn into instruments of torture and regret. Each living being eventually has to settle accounts with God for chances received and work accomplished."

The conversation had helped me understand a great deal about the true value of time, in all its facets.

The evening prayer service came and went, and shortly thereafter, Narcissa, Sal, and I made our way to one of the large "green halls." In accordance with its name, the hall was a miracle of green hues, with thick vine branches and leaves for benches, on which we sat. Under the light of chandeliers, a variety of flowers glinted brightly, filling the air with a delicious aroma.

Looking around at the audience, I was full of curiosity. More than a thousand people were in attendance. About twenty of them, I noticed, sat apart from the crowd, between us and the flower-covered mound that supported the speaker's lectern. I immediately asked Narcissa who they were.

"We're seated with the regular audience," she told me. "Those are the most advanced students present this evening. They've studied the subject deeply, so they've earned the right to speak. They're the only ones who can discuss issues with the Minister. One day we may be sitting there ourselves."

"Then you aren't allowed to sit with them?"

"Not this evening. For the time being, I can sit there only if the lecture is about the treatment of disturbed patients. Some of the students, though, stay for lectures on more than one subject, if they know enough about them."

"A curious way of doing things," I remarked.

"The Governor set up this system," she said. "It's the way all the lectures and classes in the different Ministries are run.

"He did it in order to keep the lectures from turning into chit-chat sessions," she continued, "where individuals don't do anything but air their own opinions. Talking about a subject requires that you know it well enough so that it's not just a waste of other people's time. Of course, if there are any doubts worth talking about or ideas that are different from the lecturer's, they usually get heard and discussed... but not until the right time comes along."

No sooner had Narcissa finished speaking than Minister Veneranda entered the hall in the company of two distinguished-looking women—Ministers of Communication, Narcissa told me. Every face lit up at the sight of her, in real accordance with the image her name had conjured up in my mind. She seemed noble, simple, unaffected.

Without any fuss, she exchanged a few words with the individuals in the reserved seating area regarding the theme and their expectations, and then started her lecture.

"As usual, our meeting is too short to allow long bursts of eloquence. I'm here tonight to talk about certain thought processes. We have with us a few hundred listeners who are still puzzled at how, in our spiritual world, there are so many objects and situations which are similar to those on the physical plane. After all, don't they know that thought is our universal language, and that mental creation plays a very important role in our lives? Yet many of these friends ask themselves questions, as they find dwellings, tools, and even the same languages as the ones spoken on Earth. That, however, shouldn't surprise anyone. We should keep in mind that, until now, we've lived in circles of dense and complex energies. Now, it's true that thought is the basis of all spiritual relations. But remember we are part of a humanity composed of millions of individuals throughout the Universe, and most of us are far from being perfectly obedient to universal laws. At the moment, we can't compare ourselves to our older and wiser friends who inhabit the Divine Spheres, but rather to the millions of individuals living in the 'lower circles' of Ego. The great teachers of incarnate humankind teach divine principles and explain eternal truths. In our lives on Earth we usually learn these laws—but don't obey them; we acknowledge the truths—but don't devote our lives to them.

"Would the admission of the power of thought raise individuals out of their inferior state? Not in the least. A hundred years on Earth represent a period of training much too short for us to become divine beings. During our apprenticeship on Earth, we learn the principles of mental energy. But we tend to forget that, for thousands of years, we've used that energy to create mental forms harmful to ourselves and to others.

"The various religions of the world provide us with training for spiritual living; but most of us only pay lip service to the things we learn from them. Words alone, however, aren't enough in performing our duties. The Bible teaches us that the God Himself moved beyond the Word, and put His creative power into action.

"We know that thought is a basic force, but we overlook the fact that we've misused this force for centuries. All of us know that parents are duty-bound to feed and sustain their own children; in the same way souls are bound to feed and sustain the ideas that spring from their dispositions. A criminal idea will produce vibrations of a noxious kind; an elevated conception will project vibrations of a heartening nature. A more concrete example might give you a better idea: water evaporates and rises high into the atmosphere, from where it returns purified. In this purified state, it now carries vital energies; and upon returning to Earth, it does so as life-giving dew and rain. However, keep that water mixed with the impurities in the soil, and it becomes a stagnant breeding ground for disease-carrying microorganisms.

"Thought is a living force everywhere. It's the creative atmosphere which involves God and His children, the Cause and its Effects, in the Universal Abode. By means of thought we, humanity, either make ourselves into angels bound for the heavenly realms, or diabolic geniuses on the road to hell. Do you see the importance of this? Of course, advanced minds, whether discarnate or incarnate, can communicate mentally without needing spoken language: thought is the basis of the mind's silent messages that, in the wonderful planes of intuition, are shared by every kind of being.

"Because this basis exists, a spirit who has lived exclusively in France can communicate, mind to mind, with an incarnate person who has only lived in Brazil. The language in which the message is articulated will always be that of the receiver, though the ability to communicate at all will depend entirely on how perfectly attuned they are. We still don't live, however, in the spheres of mental purity in which all creatures are so attuned; we are attuned to each other only in isolated groups, with the result that we are forced to continue to pursue renovating experiences on Earth, so that we can return to the spirit spheres with worthy acquisitions.

"Nosso Lar, then, is a transitional colony and a great blessing given to us as an 'extra-ordinary mercy' so that a few of us can prepare to rise to higher spheres, and the majority return to Earth with redeeming assignments. It is crucial for us to realize how important the processes of the mind are and to employ them in the best possible way from now on. Who is willing to try?"

As the lecture ended, soft music filled the air. Minister Veneranda had spoken with us for quite some time, sharing her profound wisdom and love, understanding and sensitivity. Then, without any pomp, she had ended her talk with a thought-provoking question.

"What? The lecture is over already?" I asked Narcissa, as the audience began to rise and leave.

"That's Minister Veneranda's way," Narcissa explained. "She ends her lectures while everyone is still enthusiastic. The lessons of the Gospel began with Jesus, she likes to say, but nobody knows when or how they will end."

Chapter
Thirty-Eight

TOBY'S HOME

On my third day in the Chambers of Rectification, Toby had a pleasant surprise for me. The night-shift had taken over in the wards, when he invited me to dinner with his family. As I was soon to find out, an instructive and entertaining evening awaited me.

We arrived at Toby's not long after leaving the Chambers, and he immediately introduced me to two women, one mature and the other approaching early maturity in appearance. The first was his wife Hilda; the second a vivacious woman named Luciana. Both were gracious, friendly people, and they gave me a warm welcome.

We gathered in Toby's library, a spacious room, its walls lined with shelves on which sat beautifully bound volumes (all on spiritual topics). I was reading some of the titles when Hilda invited me to come back into the garden with her to see some exquisite floral arrangements. Once outside, I saw that if this garden were any indication each residence in Nosso Lar must specialize in growing unique types of flowers. Lisias's garden, for instance, was filled with gloxinias and hundreds of lilies; here, on the other hand, banks of hydrangeas rose up from a carpet of violets. Clusters of slender trees towered over the flower banks, reminding me of young bamboo, except that the upper branches were joined by the enormous flowery boughs of a curious climbing plant that created a canopy over the entire garden. A soothing aroma filled the air.

I could hardly express my admiration at these sights, so we found ourselves talking of how beautiful the landscape was from this angle of the Ministry of Renewal. Within a few minutes our talk was interrupted when Luciana called us back into the house for a light meal.

The simplicity and cordiality of this family endeared them to me, and I would have liked to thank my host for introducing me to its members. But as had happened at Laura's, I had difficulty in finding the right words,.

We had been talking along in a friendly way for several minutes when Toby said, "My friend Andy is a newcomer to our Ministry, and probably doesn't know our family background yet."

At this suggestion I leaned forward in anticipation, and they all smiled at my interest.

"In fact, there are several families similar to ours here," Toby continued. "You see, I was married twice on Earth." And with the greatest good humor, he pointed to both women.

"Oh...oh, indeed." I stammered, trying to hide my confusion. "You mean that both Hilda and Luciana—um—shared your life on Earth."

"Exactly," he answered calmly.

Hilda turned to me. "You have to excuse our Toby, Andy," she said. "Every time we entertain newcomers from Earth he starts talking about the past."

"And why not?" Toby asked, with a laugh. "Shouldn't we be happy if we've conquered the green-eyed monster of jealousy, and come to love each other unselfishly?"

"It really is a problem that concerns all of us, though, isn't it?" I remarked. "Millions of people on Earth get married more than once. So how do you resolve those relationships here? Besides, physical death simply causes a change in form, it doesn't destroy spiritual ties—those continue through all Eternity. So what happens? Do you condemn the man or woman for remarrying? Millions are in the same boat. You know, I've often wondered about that passage in the Gospel where Jesus, talking about marriage in Eternity, promises us the life of angels."[25]

"Let's remember," Toby put in, "that, with all due respect to the Lord, we aren't in the sphere of angels yet. We're discarnate people, no more."

"But how do you solve the problem?" I asked.

----

[25] Translator's Note: Apparently an indirect allusion to Matthew 19:4-5, "For this reason a man will leave his father and mother and be united to his wife, and the two will become one flesh."

"Very simply. Between irrational animals and rational human
beings there's a series of graduated steps. There's also a huge distance to cross between us and the angels. But do we have any real
hope of reaching the level of angels if we can't even get along with
each other? Some travelers on this path have strong hearts. They're
able to exert a supreme effort of will and overcome every obstacle
they come across. But most of us can't do without a helping hand or
the loving assistance of friends and guardians. In these cases, the
solution depends on genuine fellowship, keeping in mind that real
marriage is a union of souls and can't be broken."

"However"—Luciana, who'd been quiet until now, suddenly
joined in"—it's only fair to say that our present happiness and mutual understanding is a consequence of Hilda's spirit of love and self-
denial."

"Oh, please, Luciana." Hilda protested. Her voice was humble,
but there was dignity in it as well. "Don't credit me with virtues I
don't have. Andy, you might as well learn from my experience. It
was a painful apprenticeship but, if you don't mind, I'll try to sum-
marize it for you."

She sat back and took a deep breath; I could see, by the expression
on her face, the whole story flooding back into her memory:

"Toby and I were married when we were very young," she began.
"We felt a deep affinity for each other—a spiritual connection we
both saw as sacred. I don't think I have to describe the happiness of
two people who are joined by real love and marriage. But death
seemed jealous of that happiness, and I died giving birth to our second child. Our grief was undescribable. Toby cried constantly, hope-
lessly, and I couldn't control my own despair any better on this side."

"I spent many sad days in the Lower Zone. None of the pleas and
urgings of my spiritual friends and guides got through to me.
Instead, I clutched at Toby and the two children. I wanted to fight,
like a mother hen protecting her chicks. But I realized Toby was in a
bad situation. He had to reorganize his life and our home, and provide the children with a mother's care, which they needed badly. It
wasn't easy. He asked his sister for help, but she was single and
couldn't stand children. The same was true of the cook, who only
pretended to like my children. After that he brought in two young
nurses, one after the other, but they weren't reliable, either.

"Finally, things became unbearable for Toby. He had to make a decision—the situation had become urgent—and so, a year after I died, he married Luciana. Oh, I fought against it at first, you'd better believe—I was like a wounded animal! I was so ignorant then. I struggled against the poor girl and even tried to hurt her. It was then that Jesus, in His great mercy, let my maternal grandmother pay me a visit. She had passed over many years before and I was astonished to see her arrive. In the beginning, she acted so casual, so relaxed, as if there was no special reason for this visit. But before I knew it she'd sat down and put my head on her lap, just as she did when I was a little girl. 'Well now, child,' she said, 'what's your role in life? Are you an animal or an individual who is aware of God? Don't you see that Luciana is acting as a mother to your children? She keeps your house, she tends to your garden, she puts up with your husband's moods. Don't you think she's good enough to be his partner for the time being? Is this how you show your gratitude for God's generosity? Is this the way you treat the people who serve you? You find Luciana acceptable as a caregiver to your children but despise her as a human being, as a sister? Oh, Hilda—my poor, Hilda—you've forgotten Jesus's teachings.'

"At that point, I threw my arms around her neck and cried my heart out. And very gradually, in her company, I learned to say good-bye to my old home, and a short time later I came to serve here in the colony. In time Luciana became like a daughter to me. I started devoting all my energies to serious study and to the improvement of my inner self. Toby raised another family, and because of the spiritual bond between us, they became mine, too. I learned a new lesson—to help everyone in my old home, no matter what their earthly relation to me was. Eventually, Toby joined me here, and finally Luciana arrived, so our joy was complete. And that's our story, Andy."

"Only Hilda didn't tell you how much she had to put up with while she taught me by her example." Luciana added.

"Oh pooh, now," Hilda objected with a laugh, and she gently stroked Luciana's hand.

"Thanks to Jesus—and Hilda," Luciana went on, "I have learned there are different kinds of marriages—marriages of love, of true fellowship, of readjustment, of duty... The day Hilda accepted me—she gave me a kiss on the cheek and all of the past feelings were dissolved—I felt my heart break away from the monster Jealousy. Spiritual marriages, you see, forge bonds among souls. All the others, even though they're sacred, are actually only bonds of duty; we need them to make readjustments that help clear up our past mistakes or to go through a process of redemption."

"And so we've organized our new home based on true friendship." Toby added.

"And how are marriages arranged here in the colony?" I asked.

"Through the right vibrational combinations," Toby explained, "or, to put it another way, through the maximal or complete attunement of two individuals."

At this point, my curiosity got the better of me and I forgot my manners.

"But what's Luciana's position in the family, exactly?" I asked.

"When I married Toby," said Luciana, who apparently took no offense at this intrusiveness, "I knew he was a widower, and I should've realized that our marriage would, above all, be mostly one of fellowship. But I suffered a lot before I understood that. When a couple suffers from restlessness, misunderstandings, and loneliness, you have to conclude that their marriage is only a physical union, not a spiritual one."

I had another question, yet didn't know how to put it without stepping over the bounds of good taste even further. Hilda sensed my thoughts.

"Oh, don't worry, Andy," she said with a smile. "Luciana already has a spiritual marriage partner and has been with him through many earthly lifetimes. He returned to the physical sphere a few years ago and she'll be following him next year. I think the happy meeting will be in São Paulo."

At this news all of us smiled together. Indeed, we would indeed have continued our talk at much greater length, but as Toby was called to the Chambers of Rectification to attend to an emergency case, our pleasant little talk ended abruptly.

Chapter
Thirty-Nine

*C*ONSULTING LAURA

*T*oby's case had impressed me a great deal. That household, where members were united based on principles of fellowship, came back to my mind again and again. I still considered myself the head of a household on Earth, and could imagine how hard it would be if I found myself in the same situation. Would I have the courage to follow Toby's example? I doubted it. I couldn't see myself demanding so much from Celia, and I knew that I'd never be able to accept such an imposition from her.

These thoughts tormented me and I couldn't find a satisfactory answer. I felt so confused that the next day I decided to pay Laura a visit during my free time and consult her. By this time, I trusted her as if she were my own mother.

The family welcomed me back with open arms, but they were all so busy that I had to wait for the right opportunity to talk to Laura. At last, though, the young people left for their usual evening of activities, and I found myself alone with her. I was a bit embarrassed and stumbled around for words for a time, but finally got it out. As usual, with an understanding smile, she gave me her full attention.

"You were right in coming to me," she said. "Any time we have soul-searching difficulties, we need experienced advice from someone. To tell you the truth, Andy, Toby's situation is a pretty common arrangement here, and in other spiritually evolved communities, too."

"But doesn't it shock you?" I asked, eagerly.

"Strictly from a human point of view," she replied, "these things might look sordid, Andy. But we have to consider, above everything, the principles of our spiritual nature. We have to keep in perspective the sequential nature of our growth. We all underwent a long period of animalized existence, and can't expect to get rid of every trace of it all at once. Centuries go by before we're able to rise up from the lower strata, and in that ascent the meaning of sex takes us the longest to understand. For the moment you're not going to find it easy to understand the evolved aspect of the household you visited yesterday. But you can be sure of one thing: a great deal of happiness exists in that home, and that's due to the understanding that unites the performers in this drama, which began on Earth. Not everyone succeeds in replacing chains of darkness with rings of light in as short a time as these three."

"But is that a general rule?" I asked. "Does every individual who's been married more than once reorganize their family life here so that it includes everyone they've shared their lives with on Earth?"

"Well, don't be so extreme." Laura laughed; she was a patient teacher. "Take it slow, Andy. Now, lots of people develop affection for each other, but that doesn't mean they are real partners. You must remember that vibrational affinities are much more important here than they are on Earth. Toby's case is an example of the victory of true friendship, a victory won by three individuals who made a giant effort toward an evolved understanding. This success, however, requires that the laws of fellowship and mutual respect be obeyed.

"The darker regions of the Lower Zone are filled with spirits that failed relationship trials such as the one Toby's family went through. As long as they go on hating each other, they're like unsteady compass needles moving in the direction of every antagonistic influence they come across. Likewise, if they don't understand the truth, they will be under the rule of self, and unable to enter regions of enlightened spiritual activities. There are many, many individuals who suffer for years without spiritual relief, simply because they refuse to conform to the laws of true fellowship."

"What happens then?" I asked. "If they can't receive the assistance of a noble organization, where do they live?"

"They experience the torments of their own woeful mental creations," she replied, "and then go back to Earth to re-start the lesson they couldn't learn on the spiritual plane. Divine Mercy gives them new bodies and forgetfulness of the past. They then connect, through blood ties, with the ones they deliberately shunned through hate and intolerance."

"It helps us," Laura added, "to realize and appreciate the higher meaning of Jesus' advice when He tells us to reconcile with our ene- mies as soon as possible—that's advice we all ought to follow for our own good.[26] People who use their time wisely can, when their lives on Earth are over, attain sublime spiritual achievements, and do a lot for their peace of conscience. Once they reincarnate the difficulties will be fewer and lighter.

"Many individuals spend centuries trying to undo hatred and resentment during their lifetimes on Earth and then go right back to them once they've re-entered spiritual life. The problem of genuine forgiveness with Jesus in the heart is crucial, and can't be given lip service. To forgive and really mean it is more than just a matter of words—we have to dig deep into ourselves and pull out all the poi- sons that dominated us in the past."

Laura was silent for a moment, perhaps thinking of how far- reaching were the consequences of the ideas she had just uttered.

"The experience of marriage," I said when she had turned her eyes to me again, "is very sacred to me."

"To individuals still at the simple animal stage," she continued, "our conversation would be a bore. But those of us who already know of enlightenment in Christ have to consider not only the expe- rience of marriage but also our entire sexual life, since it has an enor- mous impact on our souls."

My wife had always held a sacred place in my heart; my love for her was the strongest feeling I had ever had for anyone. Still, at these words, I remembered sexual experiences that I had had as a young man and couldn't help blushing. Laura had brought to mind the time-honored words of the Old Testament: "You shall not covet your neighbor's house. You shall not covet your neighbor's wife, or his manservant, or his maidservant, his ox or donkey, or anything that

----

[26] *Translator's Note: Matthew 5:24-25 "Therefore, if you are offering your gift at the altar and there remember that your brother has something against you; leave your gift there in front of the altar. First go and be reconciled to your brother; then come and offer your gift."*

belongs to your neighbor."[27] Now, thinking of Toby's case and how he was dealing with it, I had nothing more to say, feeling uncomfortable. Laura sensed my embarrassment.

"When we all have to work to change a particular wrong," she said, "we need a great deal of understanding from one another, and a proper respect for God Who gives us so many chances to work through those changes. For those who already have some spiritual enlightenment, Andy, every sexual experience takes on a tremendous importance. That's why no one can complete a truly redeeming program without unconditional understanding and acceptance of the human experience. Not long ago I heard a highly evolved instructor in the Ministry of Elevation say that, if he could, he'd materialize himself on Earth to teach the representatives of all religious denominations that, before it can be divine, all love has to be based on the unity and togetherness of the human community."

Our talk was at an end and Laura invited me to go up with her and see Lois, who was still confined to her room, though she had improved considerably. My visit was short, however; I had to return to the Chambers of Rectification. There I lost myself in thoughts about all I'd seen and heard that day. Toby's conduct was no longer much of a concern to me, nor was the behavior of Hilda and Luciana. What took the place of those thoughts was true awe at the all-encompassing issue of human compassion.

----

[27] *Translator's Note: Exodus 20:17*

Chapter Forty

*A*S YOU SOW, SO SHALL YOU REAP

I didn't quite know how to explain my desire to visit the Women's Department of the Chambers of Rectification, but I spoke to Narcissa about it anyway, and she offered to take me there herself.

"When God calls us to a certain place," she said, "there must be some job for us to do there. Everything has a purpose, Andy... remember that, especially during apparently 'casual' meetings or visits. When our thoughts are keen on doing good, it won't be hard for us to pick up on a divine suggestion when it comes along."

Later on that day, the two of us went to search out Naomi, the superintendent of the Women's Department, a worker of great prestige in the Chambers. She wasn't hard to find.

We entered a Department ward filled with row after row of women. They rested in immaculately kept beds, but were all pitiful wrecks. Here and there a heart-rending cry would go up; a word uttered in agony would find its way to our ears. It was in this ward that we came upon Naomi.

She radiated the same kindness as Narcissa. Her welcome was brief but cordial.

"I suppose you must be accustomed to scenes like these by now," she said to me. "It's about the same here as in the Men's Department."

Then, turning to the nurse, she said, "Narcissa, show Andy any of the sections you think may be instructive for him. Please feel free to visit any area."

As we walked around we started talking. The topic of conversation soon turned to human vanity and how it always seems to lead us into a preoccupation with material desires. We even recalled a number of teachings and well-known sayings on the subject.

After a while our wanderings brought us to Wing Seven. There, as elsewhere, rows of women lay in a long line of evenly spaced beds.

For a brief moment I stood studying the faces of these poor women; then, unexpectedly, one of them caught my eye. She had a bitter look on her face, and seemed prematurely old and worn out. Her lips twitched convulsively, with a kind of anguish that suggested surrender and yet a sense of irony at her situation. She had extremely bad eyesight; in any case her eyes looked dim and troubled. I thought I recognized her. But who in the world could she have been? I started searching my memory, feeling more and more heavy-hearted as I went along. Then, I remembered.

Her name was Lisa—a Lisa I'd known years ago when I was a young man. Her suffering had changed her—that was very evident—but once her image, as she had been then, formed in my mind, there was no doubting her identity.

I remembered perfectly the day I first met her. One of my mother's old friends had brought her, a young and humble-looking girl, to our house as a possible servant, and Mother had taken her on. Initially our relationship wasn't anything out of the ordinary, but over time it progressed. The line between employer and employee vanished and we grew more and more intimate. Lisa was a wild young woman, experienced in ways that I was not —until our acquaintance, that is —and when we were alone, she used to tell me about her previous escapades. With that, whatever self-restraint still existed between us broke down.

One day, my mother had a serious talk with me about the situation. This kind of intimacy wasn't a good thing, she warned. Being kind and generous to Lisa was all very well; but our relationship shouldn't go beyond that. It was too late, though. I had taken advantage of her and of the circumstances as much as I could. Not long after our talk, Lisa, who didn't have the courage to accuse me to my face, opted to leave the job and our house.

Time passed, and the incident became a faded memory for me. Like everything else, however, it wasn't blotted out of my mind. Now here was Lisa, crouched in a bed before me, cowed and miserable. Where had this poor creature lived after that turbulent episode in her early life? Where had she been? Clearly, this wasn't a case like

Silva's; in that fiasco I shared the responsibility with my father. Here, whatever debt existed was all mine. I felt nervous and ashamed by all these reminiscences. I felt like a child anxious to be forgiven for wrongdoing. I turned to Narcissa for guidance.

As I began speaking, I thought of the trust these wonderful women always seemed to inspire in me. I would probably never have had the courage to ask Minister Clarence the kinds of questions I'd put to Laura, and I knew, given the present situation, that I'd have acted very differently if I'd been with Toby. But a generous and loving woman has always a motherly sensitivity, and so I opened my heart to Narcissa. She seemed, by her expression, to understand everything. No sooner had I broached the subject than tears began to well up in my eyes. Halfway through my confession Narcissa interrupted me.

"Don't say another word, Andy. I can guess the rest of it. Don't give in to disturbing thoughts like this. I know how you are torturing yourself, from my own experience. However, the Lord has given you the chance to meet this woman again, and it has to be because you're in a condition to repay your debt."

She stopped, but sensing my indecision, spoke up again, throwing out an anchor to me. "Don't be afraid," she said. "Go to her. Try to comfort her. Remember, Andy, in time we always come across the fruits of the trees we've planted, whether they're good or bad. That isn't just a phrase from a book, either—it's a reality for everybody. I've learned a lot from situations just like this one. You're a debtor right now. Debtors who are willing to settle their debts are blessed."

She saw that I had already made up my mind to atone for the wrong I had done, so she added, by way of advice, "Go on now. Don't tell her who you are for a while. Leave that for later, when you've managed to help her a bit. It won't be hard—she'll be almost blind for some time yet. I'd say, by her aura, that she was one of these poor fallen women and a failed mother."

We went over together to where Lisa was lying; I began to talk to her in as soothing a tone as I could. She told us her name, and said she'd been brought to the Chambers three months before. Right then, I decided to humble myself before Narcissa so that the lesson would be permanently written in my heart.

"You must have suffered a great deal, Lisa," I said. "Was your life really so bad?"

She sensed the underlying affection and caring in my voice and smiled a small, resigned smile.

"Oh, why call up all these sad old things?" she returned.

"Hard experiences are always powerful teachers." I replied, trying to encourage her.

Lisa, I could see, had been defeated in the moral battle. She reflected awhile, as if conjuring up the past.

"I wasted my life," she began. "Every woman does the moment she decides to trade a life of work for a life of illusion. I was born into a dirt-poor family, so when the chance came along to go into service in the house of a wealthy businessman, I jumped at it. From that moment on, my life underwent a tremendous change. I was still very young, and the businessman had a son about my age. The son and I gradually developed an intimate relationship—to the extent that I couldn't stop it and had to leave the family. Afterwards, I forgot that God never denies work to anyone who wants to lead a worthwhile life. Instead, I found myself involved in a series of sick adventures that I won't go into. I tasted the good life—material comforts, luxury, pleasure. These were followed by extreme anger at myself, veneral disease (syphilis), a public hospital, and rejection by all my friends. I was more disillusioned than ever. In the end I went blind, and then came physical death. For the longest time I wandered, I don't know where; but I was as despondent as I'd ever been. Then one day I prayed to the Blessed Virgin with such passion that, for Her sake, some heavenly messengers rescued me and brought me here, where I've gotten so much help."

"And who was the man who pushed you into this life?" I asked, my eyes full of tears.

She said my name and that of my parents.

"Do you hate him?" I asked, anxious and embarassed.

"I blamed him for all my past sufferings," she admitted. "I had a mortal hatred for him. But Sister Naomi has helped me change all that. I see now that hating him can only mean that I'd have to hate myself, because both of us share the blame for what happened. So I can't make accusations against anyone."

This humility on Lisa's part touched me so much that I took her hand. Guilt at what I had done overwhelmed me. Tears rolled down my cheeks and onto that hand.

"Listen, Lisa," I said in a broken voice, "my name is Andy, too, and I want to help you. From now on you can count on me. I'll do everything I can for you."

"Your voice...that voice," she said, "your voice also sounds almost like his ..."

"Until now," I went on, "I haven't had a family here in Nosso Lar. So from now on you'll be my sister, and you can count on me to be as devoted as a real brother — I'll be someone you can always rely on."

"Oh, thank you, thank you, Andy!" she exclaimed. She dried her eyes, and a radiant smile spread across her face. "It's been such a long time since anyone has comforted me or spoken kind words to me. May Jesus bless you for it."

And at that moment, Narcissa, seeing that my tears were now preventing me from speaking, took both my hands in hers, and repeated Lisa's words in her motherly way, "Yes, Andy, may Jesus bless you."

Chapter
Forty-One

A CALL TO THE BATTLEFIELDS

*I*n the first days of September 1939, Nosso Lar began to suffer the impact of the conflict just then breaking out on Earth, as did other spiritual colonies associated with the American civilization. World War II was around the corner, and it would be just as disturbing in the spiritual world as it would be destructive on the physical one. In the Chambers, we talked a great deal about the war amongst ourselves. Most of us, I need hardly add, couldn't disguise our horror.

For a long time, we knew, the great spiritual communities in the East had been facing hostile vibrations from Japan. For me, new lessons were starting to unfold. Now we began to see signs that our spiritual colony would also be affected. Just as the spiritual circles of Asia were acting in silence behind the world scene, Nosso Lar started gearing up for the same kind of work. The Governor issued appeals touching on good fellowship and empathy; he especially emphasized the need to watch over our thoughts with special care, and to curb our negative impulses. I soon understood that superior spirits, in these circumstances, look on aggressors not as enemies but violators of order whose abusive actions must be stopped.

"Unfortunate are the people who intoxicate themselves with the wine of evil," Sal said to me one day. "The victories they may win are temporary, and all they've done is taken steps toward their ruin; they will become instruments of their own final downfall. When a nation causes war, it introduces disorder into the House of God and it pays a steep price for it."

I began to see that any time ignorance and darkness join to spread anarchy and destruction, the superior circles of life converge to defy such attack. An aggressor country, my fellow workers told me, naturally transforms itself into a powerful nucleus around which forces of evil gravitate. Its people, except for the high-minded individuals among them, ignore the great dangers they're incurring, calling up perverse forces from the dark regions, and doping themselves with their poison. Whole sections of society become instruments of crime. Legions of evil-minded spirits work their way into the great centers of economic progress, turning them into places of cruelty and horror. But that isn't the whole story—because, even as the forces of darkness invade the minds of that country's populace, spiritual legions from evolved worlds quickly arrive to build resistance in countries under attack. I found myself thinking what a pity it all is. For if we are to feel sorry for the individual who violates the Law of fraternity, we should feel all the sorrier when an entire nation fights it.

Late one afternoon, a few days after the first bombs had exploded in Poland, I was in the Chambers of Rectification with Toby and Narcissa when we heard, for more than fifteen minutes, the unforgettable call of a great trumpet blaring all around us. At the sound, powerful emotions gripped us, and we stood looking at each other—saddened, anxious, amazed.

"It's a call from advanced spheres—urging us all to participate in emergency services to help Earth," Narcissa explained.

"It's the sign that war couldn't be avoided," Toby added, his voice reflecting profound concern. "It'll be fought with terrible consequences to humanity. And the Americas won't be insulated. Although the two continents are an ocean away from each other, America had its origins in Europe."

A profound silence fell over the entire Ministry of Renewal with the exception of the trumpet, which sounded on and on, producing strange, soul-stirring tones.

"When the trumpet sounds in the name of Divinity," Toby explained, noticing my anxiety, "we should stop all noise down here so that we can hear its appeal in the depths of our hearts. It's sounded by spirits on a very high plane."

The last notes of the mysterious instrument at length died away, and the three of us went out into the great park and looked up into the night sky. Countless points of light spread above us, shining in the darkness. Later, as we returned to the Chambers, we heard loud noises coming from the streets. Toby left Narcissa in charge of several patients and invited me to come see what was going on in the busy avenues. Once outside, we made our way toward Government Building Square; through all the departments we passed, I noticed signs of movement and intense activity. Large groups of people seemed to be everywhere and all headed in the same direction. I was perplexed.

"All of these people are going to the Ministry of Communication for news," Toby explained. "The trumpet call we just heard only sounds when the situation is extremely serious. We know it has to do with war, but the Ministry of Communication may have some of the particulars for us. Look at that group going by—"

Two men and four women were walking beside us, talking in excited voices.

"Can you imagine what'll happen to us workers at Assistance?" asked one woman, "We've already received a record number of petitions—and this has been going on for months. It's been really tough to keep up with all the work."

"Well, what about us in Renewal?" the older of the two men put in. "Our work-load has seen a huge increase. And on top of it all, the general alert against negative thought patterns coming from the Lower Zone is going to demand constant effort from everybody in my department."

Toby touched me lightly on the arm.

"Let's go hear some of what the other groups are saying," he whispered.

Not far away we heard two men talking.

"Do you think the European war will affect all of us?" one asked.

His friend, who seemed to be a well-grounded person, replied, "I don't see any reason to jump to hasty conclusions at the moment. Right now there's nothing new but an increase in work, and that's a blessing, in reality. Everything else seems to be taking its course. The bottom line is that sickness always teaches the value of health and disaster illuminates the path to careful introspection. But the bloodshed in China has gone on for some time and you haven't let on that you were worried in the least."[28]

---

[28] *Translator's Note: A reference to the Japanese atrocities in China. During the Japanese invasion of China (1931-1945), it is believed that over 30 million Chinese lost their lives.*

"Well ..." said the first man," it appears as if I'm going to have to change my entire work program."

His companion smiled. "Helvetius," he said, gently upbraiding him, "let's forget about our personal program and think of the collective one."

By this time Toby was already calling my attention to three women to our left, who were walking in the same direction as we were. It was a picturesque scene, even on this evening of anxious expectation.

"I'm terribly worried about it," said the youngest of the three. "Everado just can't return from the planet right now."

"It doesn't look like the war is going to reach the Peninsula, though, " one of her friends answered. "Portugal is a long way from the frontlines."

"Why are you worried about Everado?" asked the third. "What could happen if he came here?"

"I'm afraid he'd want me back as his wife, as if he still had rights over me," the youngest explained. "I couldn't bear it. He's so aggressive, and I couldn't put up with his cruelty again."

"Don't be silly," the second woman said, "He'd be kept in the Lower Zone, or some place worse. Have you forgotten that?"

"Poor thing!" Toby whispered to me with a smile. "She's afraid the war will free her harsh and abusive husband."

We spent a good deal of time watching the crowds in this way but finally reached the Ministry of Communication. There we stood in front of the vast buildings that house the colony's information services. Thousands waited along with us. They all wanted information and clarification of the situation on Earth. Very surprised by all this clamor and noise, I suddenly saw an older gentleman on a balcony high up in one of the buildings. He asked everyone for their attention, calling to us through the public address system. Once he had everyone's ear, he announced that the Governor would make an address in ten minutes.

"It's Minister Spiridian," Toby told me, identifying the speaker.

The noise and confusion subsided somewhat, and soon the Governor's voice boomed at us through a phalanx of loudspeakers.

"Brothers and sisters of Nosso Lar," he said. "Let us not become agitated either in thought or word. A demonstration of distress isn't constructive; and anxiety won't teach us anything. We should be worthy of the Lord's call—so let's obey the Divine Will by working quietly at our posts."

His was a clear and compelling voice, and it spoke with authority and love. The Governor's words had a powerful effect, and within an hour the crowd had dispersed. The usual calm of the colony had been entirely restored.

Chapter
Forty-Two

*T*HE GOVERNOR'S ADDRESS

*O*n the Sunday following the sounding of the trumpet, the Governor had promised that he would take part in the Ministry of Renewal's regular Gospel study meeting. The primary reason for this visit, Narcissa told me, was to set up new nurse development programs in the Ministry of Assistance as well as training centers in Renewal.

"War is a long way off from us," she said, "but we have to organize first-aid services—very special services, Andy—and training classes against fear."

"Against fear?" I asked, surprised.

"Yes, fear. You may not know this, but fear alone is capable of destroying a countless number of human lives. Fear is a powerful, extremely negative vibration, and it's as contagious as the worst epidemic. We rate fear as one of the worst enemies of the human race. Fear works in a crafty way: it settles in the deepest part of the soul and gradually corrodes the soul's strength."

This information, frankly, unnerved me.

"Don't worry about it" she said, reading my thoughts. "In emergencies like this one, the Government always places a greater value on anti-fear training than it does even on the nursing courses. Calm minds are our guarantee of success. Later on, you'll see how important these preparations are."

I had nothing to say to this explanation.

On the evening of the big day, I had the pleasure of being chosen, along with a great many others, to clean and decorate the large hall that was set aside for the Governor's address. I was understandably nervous, since I was about to meet this noble leader for the first time. But I certainly wasn't alone in these feelings; a great many of my associates were in the same boat.

At dawn that Sunday, the social life of our Ministry centered around the great natural hall. Soon special transportation vehicles from all the departments in the Ministry started arriving. The hall quickly filled up. The Great Choir of the Government Building Temple, as well as the young singers from the schools of the Ministry of Education, began the ceremony with a hymn, "Always with Thee, Lord Jesus," sung wonderfully by two thousand voices. Other hymns followed and the hall resounded with the choir's heavenly music. Flower-scented, delicate breezes seemed to murmur in response.

Since the Gospel study meeting was dedicated to Renewal in particular, the entire staff had open access to the green hall. Other Ministries were represented by delegations, and for the first time, I had the chance to see workers from the Ministries of Elevation and Divine Union, who seemed to be clothed in light itself. As for the festivities, I couldn't have imagined anything more beautiful; nor had I ever heard such music. The sublime sound of soft and uplifting melodies filled the air.

At ten o'clock the Governor entered the hall, the twelve Ministers of Renewal following behind him. I will never forget the nobility and imposing stature of that man, with his snow white hair and clear, bright eyes. His face reflected the wisdom of age and the energy of youth, the tenderness of the saint and the self-confidence of the just and capable administrator. In his glowing white tunic, he was tall and slim; yet despite his energetic stride as he crossed to the speaker's area, he leaned on a staff.

"The Governor," Sal said, noting my mystified look, "has a liking for patriarchal attitudes: he equates leadership to parental responsibility."

The Governor took his seat in the place of honor, and the children's voices rang out with the hymn "To You, Lord, Our Lives," accompanied by harps. He looked out over the thousands packed before him, and once the last strains of the hymn had died down, he opened a shining book. "The Gospel," Sal told me in a whisper. The Governor quickly thumbed through the pages and finally stopped at one. "You will hear of wars and rumors of wars, but see to it that you are not alarmed. Such things must happen, but the end is still to come."[29]

He invoked Christ's blessing, his voice amplified by loudspeakers, and after acknowledging the representatives of the various Ministries, addressed himself in particular to our workers. It's impossible to describe here the gentle intonation of that voice which, in its loving and compelling nature, was so unforgettable. Nor can I adequately put on paper the magnificent purposes to which he turned his comments on the Gospel, inspired as he was by his veneration for sacred things. I will, however, reproduce a few words from the end of his speech, addressing the workers in Renewal that Sunday.

"Brothers and sisters whose work most closely connects to activities on Earth," the Governor said. "I make my personal appeal particularly to you, and expect much of your dedication to our cause. Let's give the best of ourselves in courage and service. The legions of darkness are now increasing the difficulties in the lower spheres; it's essential that we kindle new lights to dispel the shadows that, through the influence of those spirits, obscure Earth at this moment. It is to you, the workers of this Ministry, that I dedicate this meeting, and in you that I place my heart-felt trust. I address not our brothers and sisters whose hearts already serve in the higher spheres, but you, who still carry some of the world's dust on your sandals.

"Nosso Lar needs thirty thousand workers trained in defense service who are willing to give the best of themselves while the battle is being waged against the forces of ignorance and crime. There will be plenty of work for all of you in the regions that separate the lower planes and our spiritual colony. We can't wait at our gates for the enemies of peace to arrive. Prevention must be active in our communities for the preservation of internal peace. We in Nosso Lar comprise more than one million individuals devoted to serving higher designs and to working for our own moral improvement. Would it be fair and just, then, to allow the colony to be invaded by millions of rebellious individuals? No—we can't hesitate when it comes to defending the common good.

----

[29] *Translator's Note: Matthew 24:6*

"I know many of you are thinking of Jesus at this moment. Yes, Jesus gave himself up to rioters and fanatics so that we could be redeemed; but He didn't abandon the world to chaos and ruin. We should all be ready, as was He, to make individual sacrifices: we can't surrender Nosso Lar to wrongdoers. Our basic concern here is true friendship, peace, love and care for others. To us, evil is a waste of energy; crime, a disease of the soul. We must keep in mind that this community is a gift from God, and we have to protect it with all our hearts and souls. What we can't save through our efforts, we aren't worthy to have or enjoy. So let's prepare everyone we need to go on missions of brotherly love to Earth, the Lower Zone, and the Regions of Darkness where our workers can teach, help, and comfort others. First and above all, however, this Ministry must organize a special defense group to safeguard our institutions and its borders."

He went on for a long time, underscoring how important it was that certain essential measures be carried out, interpreting ideas of such depth that I would never be able to reproduce them all here. Finally he ended his speech by repeating the verse from Matthew he had used at the beginning. Again, he invoked Jesus's blessing and our goodwill, so that none of us should receive the divine gift without making good use of it.

At the end, the children's choir sang a hymn Minister Veneranda called "The Great Jerusalem." As the Governor stepped down from the speaker's stand, having brought us back into an atmosphere of renewed hope, a gentle wind showered tiny rose petals upon us— wonderful petals in hues of blue that melted away as they touched our foreheads, filling our hearts with an intense joy.

Chapter Forty-Three

*A*N INFORMAL CONVERSATION

*T*he festive atmosphere lingered on at the Ministry of Renewal even after the Governor and his closest advisors had gone. We talked a great deal about the ceremony we'd just seen; and before the day was over hundreds of people had responded to the Governor's appeal and volunteered for the hard work of defense that lay ahead. I looked for Toby, wanting to ask about the possibility of following their example, but he only smiled at my innocence.

"Andy, you've just started a new job here," he said. "Don't be in such a rush to take on more responsibilities than you're ready for. The Governor just told us there'll be work for everybody. You have to remember that in the Chambers work goes on day and night. With thirty thousand workers on permanent watch, big gaps will open up in several sectors and somehow we're going to have fill them."

He could see my disappointment and added good-naturedly, "Come on, cheer up. You can always enroll in an anti-fear course. Believe me, it'll do you a world of good."

At about this time, Lisias, who had come to the festival with the delegation from the Ministry of Assistance, put in an appearance. After excusing myself to Toby, I went off to chat with him for a while.

"Have you met Minister Benevenuti of Renewal?" Lisias suddenly asked as we strolled along. "He's just come back from Poland."

"I'm afraid I haven't had the pleasure."

"Let's go find him then. I'll introduce you." Lisias sounded enthusiastic, peaceful, his voice reflecting genuine friendship and warmth. "Benevenuti has been a personal friend of mine for ages."

A few minutes later, we found ourselves in a large green park belonging to the Ministry of Renewal. Groups of visitors were scattered around the park, lounging beneath wide-branching trees, and talking. Lisias ushered me over to the largest group, where we found the Minister and several friends engaged in a lively conversation. Lisias introduced me to him with a few complimentary words. With a gesture of respectful kindness the Minister invited me into the circle of friends, without interrupting the natural flow of the conversation.

I soon discovered the topic under discussion was the situation on Earth.

"The scenes we saw were horrific," Benevenuti told the gathering. "We're used to peace in America, and had no idea of the tremendous problems involved in providing spiritual help on the battlefield in Poland; to say the least, conditions there are chaotic and difficult. The spark of faith isn't exactly alive either in the invaders or in most of the victims, who are usually prey to ghastly thoughts. Our incarnate brothers and sisters are of no help; most of the time, they just sap our strength. Since the beginning of my duties as Minister I have never seen suffering on such a scale."

"Did your delegation remain there long?" someone in the crowd asked.

"As long as we could," the Minister replied. "The delegation head, a colleague from Assistance, thought it would be better if we took advantage of the opportunity to observe and learn. We're a long way from having the power of resistance of the spiritual workers there. They're extraordinary. They have all first-aid services working smoothly, despite the depressing atmosphere, and the sickening mental energies that contaminate it. The invisible plane above the battlefield is a true hell of unimaginable proportions. Since coming back, I've realized that the human soul never shows how fallen it is, how demonic its features can be, until it is involved in a war. I saw cultured, intelligent men use all their skill to carry out what they call a "direct hit" on a civilian populace. Buildings that have taken years to build are blown up in a matter of seconds by bombs of enormous power. Along with the bombing, hateful mental creations and poisoned energies make any help almost impossible. The worst sight, however, was that of the invading soldiers at the moment of being

released from their physical bodies. Most were immediately dominated by the forces of darkness and ran away from the rescue mis-
sionaries, calling them 'ghosts of the cross.'"

"So none were rescued?" someone interrupted.

"Well," the minister answered, "one can always care for an emotionally ill person at home, but what can one do with a homicidal
maniac? Isolation is likely the only choice for them. All that can be
done is to leave them in the abysses of Darkness, where suffering
will compel them to change and to embrace new attitudes. Given the
circumstances, the rescue groups are limited to helping individuals
ready to welcome help. So there you have it—on every account what
we saw was a tragedy."

"It's hard to believe," someone said, "that Europe, all civilization
and culture, would have left itself open to such a calamity!"

"It's the lack of true spirituality," declared Benevenuti. "Well-
developed intelligence isn't enough. It is necessary to enlighten
minds and prepare them for their eternal reality. In their essentials,
all beliefs are holy and, when their ministry is in the service of Truth,
blessed. However, when the ministry is tainted by political interests,
religions fail in their mission to quench people's spiritual thirst.
Religious personalities may inspire respect and admiration for their
stands on issues, but without the divine breath they'll never communicate a single particle of faith and trust."

"But what about the Spiritist movement?" someone broke in.
"Didn't it start in America and Europe fifty years ago? It produced an
entire movement. Isn't that movement still spreading the spiritual
truth?"

"The spread of Christian Spiritist ideals is a great hope,"
Benevenuti said, holding up his hand in thanks toward the speaker.
"In every way the Spiritist Doctrine is the Comforter promised to
humankind, but it has spread slowly. It's a divine gift, but unfortunately most people on Earth still haven't seen that. The biggest percentage of new believers come to Christian Spiritism under the influence of old religious training, which is full of flaws. They want to
reap the benefits of it, but not give anything of themselves. They
appeal to the truth, but won't search it out. The more scholarly ones
often end up making human guinea-pigs out of mediums. And
many followers act as certain patients, who believe more on the dis-

ease than the cure and never stand on their own feet. To put it more concisely, there they're looking for materialized spirits to produce tricks; here we're looking for spiritualized humans to produce real work."

This little wordplay got a good-humored response from us, but when the Minister continued, his mood was more serious.

"Our task is enormous," he said, "but we can't forget that every person is a divine seed. If we keep that in our minds, we can go about our mission with hope and optimism. If we do everything to the utmost extent that we can, we can rest assured that God will take care of the rest."

Chapter
Forty-Four

*T*HE DARK REGIONS

*L*isias added to the happiness of the gathering by showing what an enormously cultured and sensitive individual he was. Not long after the Minister's talk, he took up his harp and played some old songs with the expertise of a gifted musician, reminding me of the artists I had heard in concert halls back on Earth. It all came as a total surprise to me, and as I listened, I thought to myself how each moment of this day had been more wonderful than the last, how spiritual joys had followed one after the other, as if we were in paradise. When I finally found myself alone with Lisias, I tried to convey these impressions to him. He smiled at my comments, but quickly showed me another side of his sensitive nature

"No doubt about it, when we're in the company of those we love, something happens inside us—something comforting and constructive. It's the food of love, Andy. When souls come together for a common purpose, their minds interconnect and they become centers of living force. This way everyone shares in the joy created. Naturally, the same principle applies to suffering. We live within the atomsphere that we create, inside us and around us. If we give in to sadness, we become slaves to depression; if we get wrapped up in thoughts of illness, we breed ailments in our bodies. There's no mystery. It's a law of life, and it works for both good and evil. So, in meetings inspired by friendship, hope, love, and joy we'll leave with an abundance of those feelings; but where everyone obeys the commands of selfishness, pride, and meanness, we find ourselves contaminated by depleting energies."

"You're absolutely right!" I returned. "I can see home life on Earth

is ruled by the same principles. If there's mutual respect and under-
standing in a family, life there turns into a foretaste of heavenly bliss.
If there's misunderstanding and abuse, 'home' becomes hell on
Earth."

Lisias smiled, in agreement with me.

I now took the opportunity to ask something that had been bothering me for a while.

"Lisias," I began, "in his speech, the Governor mentioned three
spheres: Earth, the Lower Zone, and Darkness. Now, I've never heard
anyone talk about this Darkness before, and I'm wondering if it's just
another name for the Lower Zone, where I wandered around myself
for a few years. We have all kinds of mentally disturbed patients from
this Zone in the Chambers. But, since you have taught me so much
about my situation and where I was when I first came to Nosso Lar, I
thought you may be able to clarify my confusion about this, too."

In his old familiar way, Lisias explained, "'Darkness' is what we call
the lowest regions we know. Let's look at it this way: all humans are
travelers in life. A very few, the ones who are aware of the divine
essence in themselves, march in a straight line toward their sublime,
final destination. Most people just loiter along the roadside. They are
millions who spend centuries repeating the same old experiences.
Instead of moving in a straight line, they prefer to follow the winding
roads. They fail, they start over, they fail again; and the longer they are
caught up in the march, the more hardships they're exposed to.
However, many of those lose themselves in the forest of life, creating
for themselves a labyrinth they can't get out of by themselves. These
are the individuals who eventually wander in the Lower Zone. Even
worse, there are those who, wrapped in thoughts of extreme selfishness, inadvertently take foggy trails that land them in deep abysses,
where they remain for an indeterminate amount of time. These are
the ones who find themselves in the Darkness region. Do you see
now?"

"It couldn't be clearer," I said. I was so intrigued by the implications
that I decided to ask a few more questions.

"What about these spiritual falls?" I said. "Do they only happen on
Earth? Are incarnates the only ones who find themselves hurtling into
the abyss?"

"That's a very apt question," Lisias said after thinking for a moment." I'd answer it by saying that wherever people are, they can always throw themselves into the abyss of evil. The difference is that, in higher spheres, the individual's personal defenses are stronger, so the sharpness of the guilt is far greater."

"But it seems to me," I insisted, "that a fall like that wouldn't be possible anywhere except on Earth. Wouldn't the divine atmosphere in more evolved spheres, as well as the knowledge of truth and guidance from above, be protection enough against pride and temptation?"

"On Earth itself, of course, we find an environment divine in nature, knowledge of the truth, and spiritual guidance. But despite the trees and fields that bless their lives, human beings wage savage battles under the shade of those trees and in the flowers of those fields. Some murder by moonlight, to the holy suggestions of a starry night they show only cold indifference. Others abuse the weak while diligently studying the divine revelation. No, Andy, Earth doesn't lack for the divine presence and its works."

These words sank deep into my heart. It's true, I thought—battles are usually fought in spring and summer, just when the colors and smells of nature are at their fullest and the light of day is at its brightest. Burglars and murderers, too, prefer to do their work at night, even while the moon and stars surround Earth with an atmosphere of heavenly poetry. Most dictators on Earth are highly cultured people, but they deliberately turn their backs on divine inspiration and live only for themselves.

My ideas about the spiritual fall had changed, but I still had questions about the Darkness.

"Could you tell me, Lisias, where this zone of Darkness is?" I asked. "If the Lower Zone is an invisible extension of humanity's mental space, where could a place with so much suffering and horror be?"[30]

"Spheres of life exist everywhere," he answered. "The void you read about in books is simply a literary image. There are countless living forms, and each species moves in its own special zone of life."

Here he stopped for a moment, reflecting on what he was to say next. "Of course, in your mind" he said, having collected his thoughts,

----

[30] Translator's Note: Such a concept finds support in the scientific views of Julian Huxley who described this as an intangible sea of thought (Evolutionary Humanism, 1964, p. 80). Teillard de Chardin labeled it the noosphere. We could think of the Darkness region as a sector of this 'sea of thought' dominated by the lower thoughts of humanity.

"you placed the spirit life in circles above Earth's surface, because you weren't aware of the ones below it. But physical life teems in the ocean and the bowels of the Earth, too. Besides, we have another consideration here: there are principles of gravitation for spirits, as there are gravitational laws for material bodies on the planet.[31] Earth isn't just a playing field where we live and act and which we can disregard and misuse as we want. It is a living organism, governed by laws that will either turn us into slaves or set us free, depending on how we act. Now, a soul weighed down with faults isn't going to be able to climb to the surface of the wonderful lake of Life, is it? Let me put it a little differently. A free bird can rise to great heights; but when it gets entangled in a mass of reeds, it's going to find taking off and flying very difficult. And when the bird gets splashed with mud, it will hardly flap its wings, and will become a prey of circumstances. Do you grasp my point?"

He didn't need to ask that last question. Suddenly, the enormous scope of the lowest zones of life, and all the redeeming struggles going on there, flashed before my spiritual eyes.

Once again Lisias stopped, thinking carefully about what he would say.

"We carry, in the deepest part of our being, the potential for good or evil. Those same potentialities exist on Earth as well, designed both to correct the wrongdoer and open the gates of eternal life to the ones who win through. Andy, when you were a doctor on Earth, you learned that the human brain has certain structures that control the sense of direction. Now you know that, in essence, these structures are governed by the spirit, and are not the product of the brain. That should help you understand my point. If you live exclusively in the dark caverns of life, your divine sense of direction becomes dim, and you end by throwing yourself into an abyss. The truth is, each of us reaches whatever destination we're walking toward."

----

[31] *Translator's Note: The author refers to different gravitational principles from those which govern material bodies in the physical Universe. On Earth, gravitation is defined as the force of mutual attraction between all bodies and is proportional to the product of the masses of the bodies divided by the square of the distance between them. In the spirit world where the spirit's physical mass is zero, attraction must be governed by different principles. It is reasonable to believe that these principles will take in consideration the individual's state of conscience, as a determinant of the density of its spiritual body.*

Chapter
Forty-Five

𝒯HE MUSIC FIELDS

𝒯hat evening Lisias invited me to come with him to the Music Fields.

"You need to relax a little, Andy," he said; then, noticing my reluctance, he added, "I'll speak to Toby about it. You know, even Narcissa takes a day off every now and then. Come on."

The idea of relaxing made me realize how remarkable was the inner change I had begun to notice in myself. Even though I had only been working in the Chambers of Rectification for a short while, I was already very attached to everyone there. Minister Gentile's daily visits, Narcissa's company, Toby's inspiring example, and the camaraderie between my fellow workers and I had greatly affected me, setting in motion a whole new direction in my thoughts and concerns. Narcissa, Sal, and I were spending all of our leisure time trying to make little improvements in the place, in order to make it cheerier and more comfortable for the patients, whom we loved dearly. Still, my relative newness to the Chambers required me to get Toby's permission to step out; Lisias and I, then, went looking for him. Lisias, in a familiar but respectful tone, did the talking, and my mentor readily agreed:

"Good idea. Andy has to get to know the Music Fields," he said, and patting me on the back, he gave me a generous send-off: "Go enjoy yourself. Come back as late as you want. Tonight, we have a full staff for a change."

On the way we stopped at Lisias's place; Laura and I, seeing each other again after a while, sat down and chatted for a few moments. Lois's mother, I learned, would be returning from Earth the follow-

ing week, and everyone in the house was overjoyed at the prospect.
I looked around the house and noticed with satisfaction that, both
indoors and out in the garden, things were more beautiful than ever.

As we left, Laura took my hand in hers and said playfully:

"So the Music Fields are going to have one more regular visitor
from now on. Just watch out for your heart, Andy! As for me, I'll stay
put for the evening. It won't be long before I find food for my soul
on Earth."

We left in a cheerful mood in the company of Polydor and
Eustacius as well as the two young women, all of whom chatted
nonstop in lively, excited voices. Not long afterwards we all boarded
the transport together, the vehicle eased into one of the squares at
the Ministry of Elevation, and we got off.

As we walked along toward the Fields, Lisias affectionately told
me: "You're going to meet my fiancée today, Andy. I've told her all
about you."

"You know, it's funny to hear you say that you'd get engaged
here. I thought that was only a custom on Earth".

"Why so?" he replied. "You tell me, Andy—does love live in the
mortal body or in the immortal soul? On Earth, love is like a gold
nugget hidden in a pile of rough stones—that is to say, it gets so
mixed in with people's needs and desires and instincts that they
have a hard time telling it from an ordinary pebble."

"Yes, that makes sense," I agreed.

"In fact," he went on, "an engagement is much better in the spiritual sphere because our senses aren't fooled by the illusions that
couples on Earth have to contend with. Our real selves show
through.... In reality, Lavinia and I have failed on several occasions
in our past experiences on Earth. Most of the blame, I admit, falls on
my shoulders, and has been the result of my thoughtlessness and
lack of self control.

"On Earth we men still don't really understand the freedom that
social law gives us, and don't use it to our spiritual advantage. Just
the opposite, in fact. We're more likely to abuse this freedom, which
leads us in the other direction, toward animality. Women have had
another experience. Up to now, they've had the advantage of being
subjected to a much sterner discipline. On Earth, they've very often
had to put up with oppression from men, and have been taught to

answer to our demands. Here, values undergo readjustment—we all see that we aren't really free until we learn to respect the rules. It seems paradoxical, I know, but it's the absolute truth."

"Are you two planning future experiences on Earth together?"

"We sure are. I still have to learn many different things, and there are debts to Earth to pay off—a considerable number, I'm sorry to say. Anyway, I suspect we'll be going back in about thirty years. In the meantime we plan to settle down here in a little house of our own."

We soon arrived at the Music Fields. The Fields—in effect, a large park—could have come from a fairy tale. Lights of multiple hues shone everywhere, and bright fountains spouted streams of water that created cascading designs in the air, wonderful to see.

It was a totally new experience for me, and I was about to declare my admiration at the sights when Lisias spoke before I could. "Lavinia always comes here with both her sisters," he said. " I was kind of hoping you'd make a good escort for them."

"Why, Lisias," I protested, giving him a doubtful look, "you know very well I'm still married to Celia."

He burst out laughing.

"Well, Andy, you do take the cake! Don't worry, I'm not trying to lead you astray. In the absence of your wife, though, you shouldn't let your marriage turn you into a hermit. Have you forgotten what it's like just to be someone's brother?"

I was slightly embarrassed at this mild reproof, and to hide it, I laughed, too. In another moment we were at the park's entrance; Lisias got our tickets and we went in. Ahead of us, I saw a large group of people gathered around an elegant gazebo where a small orchestra played light, easy, rhythmic music. Pathways lined with flowers stretched out before us in several directions, all leading, Lisias told me, to the park's center. Noting my liking for the songs, Lisias told me a little of how the park was laid out.

"At the outer edges," he said, "the orchestras play several styles of music that are geared to the personal preferences of different groups—groups, let's say, which still have not developed the taste for the most sublime music. In the center, however, you'll come across universal music, divine music, the art in its higher and holier forms."

And indeed, after we'd walked for awhile down one of the paths,
where each kind of flower seemed to exist in a kingdom all its own,
I began to catch notes of an exquisite melody. On Earth, I had
noticed that only a small number of people cared for fine music; the
rest liked the popular tunes. Here the opposite was true: the center
of the park was crowded. And what I saw there went far beyond any
other gathering I'd been to in Nosso Lar, including the festival to
honor the Governor that was held at our Ministry.

It filled me with awe. Nosso Lar's society was magnificently represented. And yet I realized the scene wasn't dazzling due to anyone's luxury and lavishness, but to the unique nature of the attending individuals—the way they had managed to combine simplicity
and beauty. Women were refined, elegant, and avoided any excess in
their clothing and accessories which might have detracted from the
divine purity they obviously strove toward.

Nor was this the only difference. The boughs of great trees, dif-
fering in size, shape and color from trees on Earth, hovered over us.
Along the flower-lined paths, couples in love walked arm in arm.
Here and there, groups of individuals held animated discussions
about subjects that touched on the highest topics. I felt insignificant
in the midst of that select gathering, and yet I was also aware of a
silent and genuine empathy with those around me. That was the
prevailing mood. Every now and then, I would hear parts of discussions that concerned Earth, but I never detected a hint of malice or
criticism. Love, the world of culture, scientific research, philosophy
made up the entire talk of these individuals, who considered each
subject in an atmosphere ripe with understanding and goodwill,
and an absence of clashes of opinion. Those with greater enlightenment lowered the vibrations of their intellectuality, and the less brilliant tried to raise theirs—all without feelings of superiority or envy.
Most groups had members who referred often to Jesus and the
Gospel, but always—and this impressed me the most—in a context
of joy. Nobody spoke of the Master by dwelling on pointless sorrows. They referred to Him instead as the supreme Teacher, the
instructor of realms visible and invisible, a spirit full of understanding and compassion, and as one imbued with the energy and vigilance needed to preserve order and justice. It was on the whole an
optimistic community, the fulfillment of the hopes of many noble

thinkers on Earth, and I was thoroughly charmed by it.

The music enraptured me, and Lisias, the superb musician, was quick to comment on it.

"Our musicians, in perfect harmony, absorb rays of inspiration coming from higher spheres. In this sense, they are like many of Earth's great composers, who are sometimes brought to circles such as ours where they pick up melodies and musical ideas which they reproduce for human ears, after adapting and transforming them with their own genius."

"The Universe, Andy, is filled with the beautiful and the sublime. The eternal and shining rays of Life reach out to us from God, Who is their source."

At that moment, a group of graceful young women joined us— Lavinia and her sisters—and Lisias ended his explanation rather quickly so that we could welcome them.

Chapter
Forty-Six

A WOMAN'S SACRIFICE

*O*ne year went by. In that time my great solace was the truly helpful work that engaged me daily at the Ministry of Renewal. Gradually I had learned how to make myself useful, to find pleasure in serving, and, imbued with those lessons, I had become happier and more confident.

I still longed to visit my home on Earth, but the opportunity to do so hadn't as yet presented itself. On several occasions I had come very close to asking permission, but each time something held me back. Hadn't the best possible help been given to me here? Didn't I have the friendship and esteem of all my fellow-workers? Besides, my desire to go home, I realized, would have already become a reality if it had been useful to me—so I decided to wait. One episode did raise my hopes greatly. I was working at Renewal, but as Laura and Toby were constantly reminding me, it was Minister Clarence at Assistance who was actually responsible for my stay in the colony. In the course of my work I met the Minister often, but he never mentioned the subject of a visit to my home on Earth. Nor did he ever change his characteristic reserve while exercising the authority that came with his duties. However, during the Christmas festivities at the Ministry of Elevation, he had touched lightly on the subject, sensing perhaps how much I missed my wife and children at this time of year. The day wasn't very far away, he told me, when he himself would go back with me to my old home. I was overjoyed at these words, and I thanked him from the bottom of my heart. Yet it was now September 1940, and my dream, still very much alive, hadn't been fulfilled....

The awareness that I was devoting my time to useful work in the Chambers was a considerable comfort. Our tasks there went on without interruption, and I worked tirelessly. I had learned to provide care and even to read patients' thoughts. I stayed in touch with poor Lisa too, and indirecly tried my best to help her in her struggles for spiritual recovery. But as my emotions gradually came into balance, my desire to see my loved ones only intensified, and my homesickness became an ever deepening source of pain. The only relief I had from these feelings came from my mother's occasional visits. It's true, she lived in a higher sphere, but she never simply left me to my fate, and whenever circumstances warranted she came to see me. The last time we met she had told me about some new plans she was working on which, as soon as they were finalized, she promised to lay out for me. That day I was greatly impressed by a new sense of strength coming from her, and I looked forward to her next visit, curious to the point of anxiety as to what these plans could be.

At last, in early September of 1940 she came to the Chambers. Her greeting, as usual, was full of love. She wasn't long in telling me, however, that she intended to go back to the physical plane in the very near future. This was the core of the plan she had been developing. The idea, in reality, surprised and upset me.

"I totally disagree, Mother," I protested. "Why should you return to the flesh? Why retread the harsh paths of the flesh when there's no pressing need for it?"

"Have you forgotten the terrible situation your father is in, Andy?" she said calmly. "For years I've worked at trying to help him, but none of my efforts have succeeded. Laertes has become a hardened skeptic, and his heart is full of poison. If he persists in that attitude much longer, he'll more than likely end up in deeper abysses. What should we do about it, then? Can you imagine not doing everything to help your father in such a condition?"

"No, of course not," I replied, considerably moved by her words. "But, Mother, couldn't you find some way to help him from here?"

"No doubt I could," she said. "But for those who really love it isn't enough to lend a helping hand from a distance. What good is it to have all the riches in the world if you can't share them with those you love? Would you be happy to live in a palace if your children couldn't even get past the door? No, Andy, I can't keep my distance anymore. But at least on this side I have you to count on now, and I feel ready to join Louisa and help your father find the way to redemption."

"But, Mother, are you sure this is the only solution?" I said after a few anguished moments of thinking about the matter.

"Yes, nothing else will work," she said. "I've looked into all my options very carefully, and my superiors agree that it's best. If I can't raise the inferior to the superior, I can do the opposite and lower myself to the inferior. There's no other way, and I can't hesitate one minute. But I will have you for support in the future. So please don't lose your way, Andy, and when you're able to move through the distance which separates Nosso Lar and Earth, give your mother all the help you can. In the meantime, don't forget about your sisters. They're still in the Lower Zone working out their problems. Yes, I'll be back in the physical world very soon. I'll meet Laertes there and together we'll carry out whatever assignment God gives us."

"Meet him?" I asked. "How? In spirit?"

"No," she answered. She looked at me then with the gravest expression I'd seen on her face that day. "Not long ago, with the help of a few friends, I started arranging for his immediate reincarnation. Last week I finally settled him in his new home on Earth. He wasn't aware that he was getting any direct help from us, of course, because we chose a time when he was trying to get away from the two women I told you about, who are still tormenting him. His mental state was distracted at the time and that was very helpful for our purposes. Before he knew what was happening, we had managed to unite him to his new physical body."

"Can you really do things like that?" I asked, very much confused at this point. "What about individual liberty?"

"Some reincarnations come about pretty drastically," she said with a sad smile. "The medicine might be bitter but it's sacred, and if the patient is afraid to swallow it, his friends just have to help him with the task. Keep in mind that a soul isn't really free until it comes to understand its duty and act on it. Besides, debtors are always slaves to their debts. God created free will, Andy; human beings created fate. We forge our own chains—and we're the ones who have to break them."

This answer gave me much to think about, but my mother was far

NOSSO LAR - A SPIRITUAL HOME

from finished.

"Needless to say, the two women aren't about to give up on him; they keep a close watch. If it hadn't been for the Divine assistance and the intervention of our mentors, they might have stopped him from reincarnating this time."

"But Mother!" I said, shocked by her words for the second time in as many minutes. "Can evil forces control us to that extent? Are we simply puppets in our enemy's hands?"

"We should ask ourselves questions like that, Andy," she returned, "before contracting moral obligations and turning our brothers and sisters against us. Never borrow what you can't pay back."

"And what about these women? What's going to happen to them?"

"Why, they're going to become my daughters," Mother continued. "Don't forget that I am going back to help your father, and I can't do that well if I antagonize them even more. You don't put out a fire by dowsing it with gasoline, do you? Love, Andy—love is indispensable. Whenever people doubt love, they abandon the right road and find themselves wandering in the desert; when they reject love they drive their lives straight into a swamp. Right now, your father is a skeptic, and those poor women are wading in ignorance and delusion. They're bending under the burden of illusions and desire and don't know how to throw them off. That's why, very soon, I'll take them into my arms and be the mother they've always needed. That's how I intend to accomplish my new mission."

Though she smiled, her tears unshed, she seemed to gaze far beyond my room and into the future.

"Later on, who knows?" she said. "One day I may come back to Nosso Lar and bring them with me, and their feelings will be very different. We'll have then a reunion full of joy and love and togetherness!"

Her self-denial was noble, filling me with awe and respect. I knelt down and kissed her hands. She was no longer just my mother to me. She was a messenger of divine mercy, someone who could take her worst enemies to her heart and change them into individuals who could retrace their steps and start again as true children of God.

Chapter
Forty-Seven

$\mathcal{L}$AURA'S RETURN

$\mathcal{M}$y mother wasn't the only one in my circle getting ready to return to the physical plane around this time; Laura was preparing for the same journey. Shortly before her departure I learned that a number of workers in the colony, especially from the Ministries of Assistance and Renewal, were planning a farewell party for her. This was to be held on the evening she received her complete service dossier from the Personnel Department.

Words can't express how spiritually meaningful that little party was for me. The house, always a charming place, was alive with music and light, and even the flowers seemed more beautiful, as if aware of the special occasion. Entire families dropped by throughout the evening to say goodbye and wish Laura well, after which most of the visitors went home to allow her a bit of privacy in her last moments with her closest friends. Those of us in that enviable category stayed late that night; and it was a blessing. During that time I had the chance to hear dialogues and observations that struck me as remarkable.

As the evening wore on, I could see that Laura grew more serious and introspective than she had been earlier. She made a great effort to join in the general optimism, and in the crowded living room talked at length with the Personnel representative.

"I'll probably be leaving Nosso Lar in less than than two days," she was saying, looking a bit wistful. "I've finished all my conditioning at the Preparation Service of the Ministry of Education. So, as you can see, I'm ready to go."

The representative, the personification of good fellowship, gave her all the encouragement he could.

"I hope you're feeling excited about this new experience, Laura" he said. "It's wonderful for someone to go back to Earth in your circumstances. You have thousands and thousands of service hours to your credit. You stand out even here, in a community of over a million. Besides, you're leaving children here and they'll be tremendous motivators to you on Earth."

"Yes, that's very comforting," she replied. Still, she couldn't manage to hide her concern over the return. She didn't look very comforted. "But we can't forget what an important undertaking reincarnation always is. Oh, I know that my husband is on Earth now and my children will be constant friends while I'm there, but nonetheless..."

"Laura, Laura! Please, my dear," Minister Gentile interrupted, "don't get caught up in speculation about what's going to happen. We have to trust in the Divine Protection, and in ourselves. Remember, there are no limits to Providence's resources. We must break those dark glasses that present the Earth journey as a painful exile. Stop concentrating on the possibility of failure and start visualizing the probability of success. Besides, you can always count on your friends over here a little, can't you? And as far as 'vibratory distance' is concerned, we won't be all that far away. Just think of the pleasure you'll find in helping old friends, and how wonderful and glorious it will be to do really useful work there."

These comments seemed to cheer her up a little. She said, "Yes, I know you're right, Minister. And I've lined up the spiritual help of my co-workers so that I can stay aware of the lessons I've learned here. Yes, Earth is filled with divine beauty—it's enough just to think that the same sun shines on Nosso Lar as on incarnate spirits. But, my dear Gentile, what frightens me is the oblivion. I know it's only temporary, but it still scares me...sometimes. I feel like a patient who's been wounded many times and who's recovered now. The wounds have healed and don't hurt anymore; but the scars are still there, and the slightest scratch might be enough to start them bleeding again."

The Minister nodded in understanding.

"I'm not trying to minimize what the fog of the physical sphere represents," he said. "But we have to summon up our courage and go on deliberately. We'll help you work hard for the well being of others, and steer you away from self-indulgence. Trust that. Remember that the great obstacle, now and always, is getting caught up in the temptations of selfishness."

"Here, of course," Laura answered, "we can always count on the positive spiritual vibrations of our neighbors and friends who are living according to the Gospel. And when our flaws creep up on us every now and then, the environment we live in becomes a natural defense. But on Earth, our good resolutions are like flickering lights in a stormy ocean."

"Oh, don't say that, Laura." said the Minister, shaking his head. "Try not to attach so much importance to the negative forces. We shouldn't give the enemy the weapons to attack us. Our minds are true battlefields of ideas. But any helpful flame we light there burns forever. The winds of human passions can blow like hurricanes, but can't blow out a single light that belongs to God."

These words took hold of Laura and, in a matter of moments, she seemed to change her mental attitude and become much calmer.

"I'm sure your coming tonight was providential, Minister," she said with new enthusiasm. "I definitely needed your encouragement. You're right, the mind is a constant battlefield. We have to chase evil and fear out of ourselves; we have to root them out and not give them importance. Yes, I can see that clearly now."

Gentile, pleased at the effect of his remarks, said, "Remember this too, Laura: within us, each idea works as if it were a separate entity. If we nurture goodness within us, all the separate ideas will come together and develop into defenses, helping us reach for happiness. The minute we start nurturing negativity, however, we start building a secure base for the enemies of our peace to operate from."

Gentile stopped speaking for the moment, whereupon the representative from the Personnel Department added, "We also have to remember that Laura's going back to Earth with extraordinary spiritual credit. Just this morning the Governor's secretary sent a note to the Ministry of Assistance recommending that the reincarnation experts take great care to ensure that her genetic endowment is excellent."

"Yes," Laura said, happy at the thought. "I asked for it so I wouldn't be too affected by heredity laws. I've been concerned with blood disorders especially."

"Well, your merit has stood you in good stead," the representative continued. "The Governor himself saw to it that your request was taken care of."

"Do you hear that, Laura?" Gentile said brightly. "Don't worry about anything—you're going to be all right." He smiled at her and nodded his assurance. "You're going to be helped by all your friends and fellow-workers. We'll be doing every thing possible for you."

"Oh thank God for that—and for you!" Laura exclaimed, and the relief was evident in both her voice and demeanor. "You've done me so much good. You've said exactly what I needed to hear."

Lisias and his sisters, including the newly arrived Theresa, were now happier and more confident themselves.

"My mother needs to forget her worries," Lisias said. "After all, we're not going to sit around dawdling while you're away!"

"You're right, dear," she agreed. "I do need to worry less. And I'll cherish my hope, and trust in the Lord and in all of you."

The rest of the evening saw a change in the atmosphere of the gathering as well, and the conversation was full of confidence and optimism. We discussed her return to Earth, how it was a blessing, a chance to review old and learn new lessons.

I took my leave quite late, but not before Laura, holding my hands in hers, said, "I do hope to see you again tomorrow evening, Andy. We're holding a family gathering here—just close friends. The Ministry of Communication promised us a visit from my husband. He's already in the flesh, but some friends are helping to bring him here. Besides, I'll be saying goodbye to all of you. So please, be sure to come."

I thanked her, my voice heavy with emotion, and tried hard to keep back the tears gathering at the thought of my sweet friend's departure.

Chapter
Forty-Eight

GOSPEL AT HOME

No follower of the Spiritist Doctrine would have been surprised at what I saw in Lisias's home that next evening, but the experience was new and interesting to me. Thirty or more people had gathered in the large living room, whose furniture had been quite unpretensiously rearranged for the occasion. Comfortable arm chairs had been placed in rows of twelve in front of a platform, behind which sat Minister Clarence, our master of ceremonies; Laura sat near him, surrounded by her four children. A six-foot tall dome had been placed approximately twelve feet away from the platform; it was apparently made of a substance like very thin crystal. The bottom part of the dome was covered with wires connected to an apparatus resembling a small loudspeaker.

As I looked around at the gathering, many questions came to mind. Visitors had already taken their seats, and I could hear conversations going on in a friendly and relaxed way among the different groups. In the seat next to me was Nicholas, a long time worker from Assistance, and I took advantage of this chatty moment to find out more about what was to take place. He answered willingly.

"We're ready now—just waiting for the OK from Communication. Richard is still in his childhood period on Earth, so it won't be hard for him to leave his physical body for a while."

"So he's really coming here?"

"Why not? Just because a spirit is incarnate doesn't mean it's chained to Earth. Some are like homing pigeons, flying back and forth between places. Living in two worlds, you might say. That dome there," he pointed, "is where he'll appear to us."

"But why inside the dome?" I asked "Can't he appear outside of it?"

"Yes, but you have to remember that our emotions can send out disturbing vibrations. The dome is made of a substance that insulates him from any discordant vibrations. It'll protect Richard from our mental energies."

That's when Lisias received the signal. It was the expected call from Communication; the meeting could begin. It was forty minutes past midnight. I pointed out the lateness to Nicholas and gave him one of my questioning looks.

"This is the only time when it's quiet enough in Richard's new home," he whispered. "The whole house has to be quiet, his parents are asleep. He's still just a baby, and at this point in his life his spirit is relatively unrestrained by physical matter."

Nicholas might have continued, but Clarence rose and asked for perfect unity of thought and a true fusion of feelings. In the ensuing silence, he offered a simple and moving prayer. Then Lisias played a beautiful melody on his lute, filling the room with enchantment and vibrations of peace.

The last notes of the song at length died away, and Clarence spoke again.

"Brothers and sisters," he said, "let's all send Richard our message of love."

At these words, Laura's daughters and granddaughter left the platform and went over to a corner of the room that was piled high with musical instruments. Lisias followed. Theresa sat at the piano, and Lois and Lisias picked up the harp and zither, respectively. Next to them stood Judith and Yolanda, who formed the little family choir. The players began with a beautiful melody that quickly lifted me up into spheres of the highest thought. In a few moments the voices joined in, very sweet in their tone; Lisias and his sisters were singing a song they had composed for the occasion. I can only give an inadequate idea of the verses, which were profoundly evocative and full of spirituality and beauty. I can only try to reproduce the lyrics, here, as a demonstration of how beautiful love can be in the spheres of life beyond death's reach:[32]

----

[32] *Translator's Note: This is an adaptation of the original poem respecting both its content and structure.*

When at last, at last the night
Brings you blessings of sweet sleep,
In your slumber, Father, keep—
Father, keep our love alight.
While the stars are twinkling far,
While a song may cause a tear,
May your heart be with us here.
Join us, join us from afar.

Let no troubles bring distress
In the road that lies ahead,
Come share in this light instead,
Let our love your heart caress;
Fear no hurt or earthly pain,
Know tomorrow will for sure
Bring us joy, forever pure
Join us, Father, here again.

While the world may give you rest,
Celestial dawns await you here.
Hope enlightens our bright sphere,
Love brings joy to our nest;
Look then to a future day
When together we will find
Friendship's garden in love entwined.
Join us, Father, here today.

Come to us, our Father dear,
Though you come to us in dreams;
Drink from Nosso Lar's bright streams,
Relive the beauty of this sphere.
Full of hope and tender care,
For a while forget the flesh;
Sip from our rich waters fresh.
Join us, join and with us share.

Father dear, we've not forgot
Your kindness, love, and sacrifice,

The clearness of your wise advice,
The Way of love that you once taught.
Come now, like the light of day—
Through the heavy shadows pass,
Flesh defeat, hilltops surpass.
Join us, join us while we pray.

As the singers came to the last lines of the song, a rich radiance began filling the dome before us. Soon the handsome figure of a middle-aged man took form—it was Richard. The emotions of the family as they welcomed him were sacred indeed, and I hardly have the skill to do them justice on paper.

At first, Richard spoke privately to his wife and children. Then he looked toward the gathering, friendly and content, and asked his children to sing the song again. As he listened tears came to his eyes. When we finished, he spoke.

"How great is Jesus's mercy," he said, obviously moved. "Tonight He has blessed our family study with the most supreme joy imaginable. We've sat together so many times in this room trying to find in the Gospel our way to a better tomorrow. Here we've often received the bread of life. Now we've gathered again with all of you and received this sacred reassurance. It makes me so very happy!"

Laura wept quietly, and the eyes of Lisias and his sisters brimmed over. Richard, I noticed, spoke with some difficulty, and evidently only had a short time to stay with us. Everyone in the room must, I think, have had the same impression.

After her father had finished, Judith put her arms around the crystal dome and said in an affectionate voice, "Father, tell us what you want us to do. How can we can help you, daddy?"

Richard looked lovingly at his wife.

"Your mother will soon be coming to join me, Judith," he said in a low, soft tone. "So will all of you, in time. I couldn't ask for anything more to make me happy. But you can ask the Master to bless us forever."

By this time tears were running down our faces. Not long afterwards, the radiance started to fade. An emotional Richard spoke for the last time:

"Children! I'd like to make a request from the bottom of my heart! Pray to the Lord that my life on Earth will never be easy, so that the light of gratitude and understanding may always burn like a bright flame in my spirit!"

Being so unexpected, this appeal surprised and touched me simultaneously. But there was no time to consider it. Richard said goodbye and prepared for his departure. Gradually, a grayish mist spread throughout the whole dome, and Richard's image disappeared. After a few minutes, the dome returned to its original clear state. Clarence then closed the meeting with a prayer, leaving us so happy that I still have no words to describe it.

Now our hostess stood on the platform, surrounded by all her guests; they crowded in, anxious to congratulate her, wish her well, and say goodbye. I did the same, and told her how deeply she had impressed me and how much I owed to her.

Someone touched me lightly on the shoulder. It was Clarence.

"Listen, Andy," he said. "Tomorrow I'll be going with Laura to the physical sphere. If you like, you can come with us and pay a visit to your family."

This stupendous news took me aback. But even as my heart leapt with joy, I remembered my work at the Chambers. The Minister immediately realized what I was thinking.

"You have a fair number of extra service hours to your credit, I believe," he said. "So Gentile will have no problem granting you a week off. After all, you've completed a whole year of active service."

I was overwhelmed with joy and thanked Clarence, weeping and laughing at the same time.

At last, I was going to see my beloved wife and children again.

Chapter
Forty-Nine

ℛETURNING HOME

*𝒥*n some ways I felt like a child being led somewhere safe and familiar by an old and trusted friend. Put another way, I arrived back in my hometown feeling like a traveler who has come home after years spent living in foreign countries. The countryside hadn't changed much; I was glad to see the neighborhood's old trees, the sea, the sky, and to recognize the same sweet scent in the air. Joy and excitement filled me at these sights and smells, and I was no longer aware of Laura's anxious, preoccupied expression.

Not long afterwards I took leave of our little caravan. It continued on, but not before Clarence had given me a warm hug.

"You have a whole week to do with as you like," he said. "I'll come and see you every day. I have to keep going back and forth to take care of some last details regarding Laura's reincarnation; so if you want to go back to Nosso Lar any time, you can come along with me. Take care of yourself, Andy."

I said a last goodbye to Laura, and in another few minutes found myself alone and deeply breathing the air of the past. I didn't, however, spend much time looking at my old neighborhood, and quickly made my way through the streets toward home. I reached the big front gate and stood before it, my heart pounding heavily. As always, the wind whispered softly through the small garden. Azaleas and roses bloomed everywhere, welcoming the spring. Near the front door stood the palm tree Celia and I had planted on our first wedding anniversary.

I was, to put it mildly, drunk with joy. But when I went into the house, I noticed that it had changed considerably. Where, I thought, was our fine old rosewood furniture? The large family portrait of Celia, the children, and me gathered around in our intimate little group—where had it gone?

What in the world had happened to everything?

Worry and anxiety overcame me, and I literally began to stagger with emotion. I went into the living room, and saw there the younger of my two daughters, who during these many years had grown into a beautiful young lady. Almost at the same moment, Celia came out of our bedroom with a gentleman who impressed me, at first glance, as a doctor.

At the sight of her, I shouted with joy with all the power in my lungs; but those shouts, which echoed all through the house, left no impression on those in the room. Suddenly I understood the situation; my disappointment was deep. I placed my arms around Celia with all the tenderness I had stored for so long—yet, all the time, she remained completely unaware of my affection. She looked anxious and disturbed, and suddenly asked the gentleman something I couldn't quite hear.

"I won't be able to make a final diagnosis until tomorrow," he replied in a hushed tone. "Pneumonia may cause serious complications when the blood pressure is as high as his. Ernest needs constant care—and total rest."

Who could this Ernest be?

I was lost in a sea of questions. Then I heard Celia plead in anguish.

"Oh, Doctor—for God's sake, save him! I don't think I could go through another widowhood!"

So there it was. She started crying and wringing her hands—it was obvious that her nerves were at a breaking point. But a bolt of thunder couldn't have hit me harder than her words. Another man had taken possession of my home! My wife had forgotten me; the house wasn't mine anymore.

Had it been worth it, I asked myself, to wait so long and be so disillusioned?

I went into our old bedroom and found it completely changed. A middle-aged man lay on the bed, clearly in a state of poor health, pale and breathing with difficulty. Three unfriendly looking spiritual beings walked back and forth beside him, doing their best to

increase his suffering.[33]
My first instinct was to despise him—this intruder who had taken my place. But I wasn't the same man I had once been. The Lord had called me to the practice of brotherly love and forgiveness. I realized the emergency of the situation, aggravated by the presence of the three nasty beings near him, but I wasn't able to get myself to do anything.

Confused and disappointed, I sat down. Celia would occasionally walk in and out of the room. It was hard for me to watch her. Each time she spoke to and soothed the man in bed with the love and tenderness she had once reserved for me. I sat through this for several hours—with bitterness, I confess. Eventually I went back into the living room.

New surprises soon followed.

My older daughter had arrived, and she sat talking to her sister. I saw, given the baby she carried in her arms, that she had gotten married. But what about my son? I couldn't imagine where he could be.

Meanwhile, in the bedroom, Celia gave some instructions to the nurse who had come to relieve her. Apparently calmer, she joined the girls.

"Mother, I came by to visit Ernest," my older daughter said, then added more thoughtfully, "but there's something else, too. For some reason, the thought of Father has been on my mind all morning. It's just a feeling and I can't really describe it, but . . . .."

She couldn't finish; her eyes filled with tears.

To my surprise and pain, Celia answered sharply.

"Please, will you stop this nonsense?" she snapped. "This is the last straw. I'm extremely worried about Ernest, and what do I get — understanding? No, I have to listen to your silly ideas. Stop indulging yourself in this old-fashioned sentimentalism. Besides, haven't I made it a rule in this house never to talk about your father? You know how it upsets Ernest. I've sold everything that ever reminded me of the past; I even had the walls redecorated. Why

----

[33] Translator's Note: Spirits of a lower condition are attracted to situations or people when there is sufficient affinity. The affinity may be determined by similarity of thoughts, or by the existence of debts of some kind. The motives of the three individuals here are not clear, but their appearance most probably arises from no deeper cause than a temporary identification of energies.

can't you help me instead of working against me?"

"It's this darned Spiritism she's involved in, Mother" said my younger daughter. "It's convinced her of a lot of foolishness. She thinks the dead can come back. Isn't that the craziest thing anybody ever heard?"

"Well, I'm not talking about religious beliefs, if that's what you mean by spiritist ideas," her sister answered, still crying. "Honestly, is it such a big crime to remember and miss Father? Don't you have any love in your hearts? Don't you have any feelings? If Father were here, Mother, his only son wouldn't be acting as wildly as he is."

"Oh, this is all so idiotic." Celia was clearly irritated by this last reference. "God decides our fate and we follow it. André is dead. Remember that, and please stop moaning about the past. There's nothing we can do about it."

I went over to my sobbing daughter and tried to comfort her, then whispered words of encouragement in her ear. In her own mind, she registered them as consoling thoughts. Here I was in a situation that had caught me completely off-guard. Finally, I started to understand why my real friends at Nosso Lar had put off my visit here for so long. Distress and disappointment were coming at me from every direction. My home might as well have been ransacked by burglars or brought down board after board by the boring of termites. Belongings, position, affection, all gone. Nothing left but the faithful heart of a daughter. I couldn't bear it. Nothing in the years of suffering and misery in the Lower Zone had caused me to cry so many tears. My heart was broken.

Night came and went. Morning found me in the same confused, painful state as before. I continued hearing words and observing actions that I could never have imagined.

That evening, as promised, Clarence came by, and finding how desperate I was, tried to comfort me in his wise and friendly way.

"I understand how you're feeling right now, Andy," he told me, "but let me be frank: I'm thankful for this wonderful opportunity to give your testimony. There's not much I can tell you—any advice I could give right now would be inappropriate. But, my dear fellow, you can't forget Jesus's teaching, reminding us to love God above all things and our neighbors as ourselves. Listen to his words and you will work real miracles of peace and understanding in life."

I thanked him and asked for his continued support. He smiled and left.

Alone in my trial, I finally had to face the bitter reality of my situation. I began to meditate on the meaning of the Gospel's command and my thoughts gradually became clearer. After all, why should I condemn Celia? If I'd been the one left alone on Earth, would I have been able to live by myself year after year? Wouldn't I have found a thousand reasons to remarry? And as for this poor, sick man, Ernest—why should I hate or resent him? In the House of the Lord, wasn't he also my brother? After all, our family might have ended up in much worse shape if Celia had turned down his marriage proposal.

At long last I had to fight and conquer my ruthless selfishness. Jesus had provided me with new sources of enlightenment, and I couldn't act anymore like the simpleton I had been on Earth. My family was no longer only my wife and three children—it also consisted of the hundreds of patients in the Chambers of Rectification. Even beyond them, it included the whole universal community of humankind. I gave myself up to this new train of thought, and as I did, true love began to flow from the wounds that had been inflicted on my heart.

Chapter Fifty

CITIZEN OF NOSSO LAR

On the second night I felt terribly tired. The value of spiritual nourishment—the food of mutual love and understanding—was becoming more and more apparent to me. In Nosso Lar I could go for several days, working hard nearly every hour, without taking ordinary meals. There the presence of my friends, their affection, the absorption of pure elements from air and water, were enough to renew me. Here, in my home on Earth, I saw nothing but a battle-field; at war, my loved ones had stopped being my friends.

I remembered Clarence's words of the night before, and they brought me a measure of peace and comfort. As I recalled them, I began, for the first time, to understand human needs. I wasn't Celia's keeper, but her brother and friend; I wasn't my children's master, but their companion on the road to spiritual enlightenment.

Laura had once told me that we should learn from the bees—treating the memory of the enlightened individuals we meet along the way as the flowers of life, extracting from them the substance of good examples so that we can one day harvest the honey of wisdom. I decided to take her advice and began by remembering my mother, who, out of love for my father, was returning to Earth and inviting into her life two unfortunate women, who would become her much-loved daughters. Similar examples occurred to me from my experiences in Nosso Lar. Minister Veneranda had been working for centuries to help the spiritual group related to her. Narcissa was serving in the Chambers for permission to return to the physical world where she intended to help her loved ones. For her part, Hilda had overcome the dragon of jealousy. And what about the many signs of true fellowship I had received from my friends? Clarence had welcomed me with the affection of a father; Laura, too, had treated me like a son; Toby had made me his brother. Each had given me something I could use in the transformation of my mental attitude.

I tried to forget the apparent ingratitude I found at home and put divine love before everything else. And to put their needs before my personal feelings. As I said, I was extremely tired, but went into the sick man's room and found his condition had gone from bad to worse; he was deteriorating by the moment. Celia stood by his bed holding his head in her arms. She was in tears.

"Ernest, Ernest, have pity on me, darling," she pleaded. "Don't leave me. What will I do if you die?"

Ernest took her hands in his. Despite his labored breathing, he whispered something with genuine affection.

I prayed to the Lord to give me the strength to be understanding and to consider this couple as my brother and sister. Celia and Ernest, I could see, loved each other deeply; if I really wanted to be their brother, I had to do everything I could to help them.

I set to work. My first tactic was to try to enlighten the three spiritual visitors who were keeping a close watch on the patient. This proved to be a difficult task, and in short order I found myself more exhausted than ever.

Then I remembered that Toby had once told me that not all the citizens of Nosso Lar needed vehicles to travel—the more evolved ones could, if they wanted, travel through space at will. They could also communicate mind to mind over great distances, using only the power of thought. Moreover, if they were really attuned to each other, they could do so at will, no matter how far apart they were.

It next occurred to me how useful Narcissa would be in this situation. I concentrated in a sincere prayer to God, then directed my thoughts to her, directly pleading for help. Mentally, I told her about my painful experience at home and my desire to help out in the current crisis. "I need your help, please, don't leave me to handle this all by myself." I said to her.

Some twenty minutes later, the unexpected happened. I was still deep in prayer when someone lightly tapped me on the shoulder. I looked up. It was Narcissa.

"I heard your call, Andy," she said, with an approving smile.

"Here I am."

I couldn't have been more astonished, or happier.

Narcissa looked around for a moment, sized up the situation, and immediately understood its seriousness.

"We don't have time to waste," she said. Immediately, she laid her hands on the patient and said a prayer. Within minutes, the gloomy figures had disappeared as if by magic. Then she turned to me.

"From here on we have to depend on nature," she said, emphasizing the last word.

Her manner was confident. She strode out of the room and then out of the house, with me in tow.

"Humans are not the only beings who can take in and give out energies," she explained, sensing how curious I was about what she was up to. "Fact is, every living thing in nature does it. In this particular case, we need trees. They're gonna be a big help to us."

Here was a new lesson, it seemed. I followed along after her in silence. Soon we came to a grove of mature trees. Narcissa stopped and the two of us entered it. At this point an event totally outside my range of experience took place. Narcissa suddenly called out to someone and waited expectantly. In a few moments, to my considerable surprise, eight spirits appeared. "Are there any mango and eucalyptus trees in this neighborhood? " she asked. They gave her the information she wanted. I hadn't the slightest idea who they could have been.

As usual, Narcissa read my thoughts.

"Those are regular workers in the plant kingdom," she explained.

"Plant kingdom?"

"That's right, Andy. Everything's got a purpose in God's House. If you need to know how to do something, sure enough someone'll come along to teach you. Have a problem? Providence will step in every time. There's only one being in the whole Creation who's really hapless: that's the reckless being who chose the path of evil."

Narcissa now quickly concocted a substance of some kind from the essential energies of the eucalyptus and mango trees, and we made our way back to the house. There, the patient absorbed the potion both through his inhalation and his skin, to which Narcissa expertly applied the mixture.

Within a few hours, Ernest had visibly improved.

Early the next morning the doctor examined him and, very surprised by the new developments, said, shaking his head in wonder, "What an extraordinary reaction! This is a real miracle, Celia, a miracle of nature!"

For the first time since I'd arrived, Celia was happy. The house was alive again. I was elated. Courage and hope invigorated my soul. I recognized the bonds that had held me so tightly to my sources of inferiority had forever been broken.

Later that day I went back to Nosso Lar with Narcissa. For the first time, I tried volitation. In a few moments, high among the clouds, we had covered an enormous distance. Between my experience at home and this new sensation of moving freely through the air, happiness unrolled in my soul like a banner. I felt wonderfully light, in body and heart, and said so to Narcissa.

"In Nosso Lar," she said, "lots of spirits could do without transport units and go around on their own like this, at least inside the colony's vibratory range. But most can't yet, so none of us do it in public. That doesn't stop us from using it outside of the colony, though, particularly when we have a long way to go and need to save some time."

Once back in the colony, I realized that a higher understanding had come to me; a new joy now enriched my heart. Narcissa gave me further volitation instruction, and making use of it, I went back and forth between my old home on Earth and the spiritual colony without a problem. In this way, I was able to intensify Ernest's treatment, to which he responded with rapid improvement. True to his word, Clarence came to visit me every day and pronounced himself satisfied with my work.

At the end of the week, my first leave of absence from the Chambers came to a conclusion. Ernest's health was restored; the couple was happy again. I looked on them now as my true brother and sister; but it was time to go back to my regular duties, and I took my leave. A magnificent sunset was just then in progress, and in its light, I left for Nosso Lar. My spirit had undergone a total change from what it had been at the beginning of my visit. In those seven short days I had learned precious and practical lessons in understanding and in love for others.

Helped along by the beauty of the early evening, my mind was filled with the most elevated thoughts I'd ever known. How great

Divine Providence is, I said to myself. How wise God is in planning our work and life situations—how loving in taking care of His creation!

All of a sudden my meditation was interrupted. Coming in my direction, I saw well over two hundred of my friends and fellow workers: Lisias, Lavinia, Narcissa, Silva, Toby, Sal and so many other workers from the Chambers—all were there. In their greetings I heard a new joy, in their welcome a new brightness of spirit. The gathering took me by surprise; and looking from one face to the other, I was at a loss as to what to do. It was then that Minister Clarence came forward. He held out his hand and grasped mine, pumping it enthusiastically.

"Andy," he said, "until today you've been my protegé in this colony. But from this moment on, in the name of the Governor, I declare you a citizen of Nosso Lar!"

My victory had been so small. Why then was I being treated so generously? What had I done to deserve it?

I couldn't hold back the tears any longer; they choked my voice. The wisdom of Divine Mercy filled my heart, and I threw myself into Clarence's arms, crying with gratitude and joy.